WHAT IS OPUS DEI?

WHAT IS OPUS DEI?

Dominique Le Tourneau

THE MERCIER PRESS

The Mercier Press, 4 Bridge Street, Cork
24 Lower Abbey Street, Dublin 1

Original title in French:
L'Opus Dei (Collection "Que Sais-Je?" No. 2207)
© Presses Universitaires de France
Paris, 1984

English translation:
  © Sinag-tala Publishers, Inc.
  Manila, July 1989

ISBN 0 85342 834 4

Nihil Obstat:
  Msgr Benedicto S. Aquino
  Vice-Chancellor & Censor

Imprimatur:
  Msgr Jose C. Abriol
  Vicar General

  Manila, March 9, 1989

The publishers wish to thank Mr Hospicio Neri of Manila for the
English translation and Mr Dennis Helming of Washington, DC for
copyediting the entire manuscript.

Printed in Ireland by Colour Books Ltd.

Contents

Introduction

The personal Prelature of the Holy Cross and Opus Dei, usually just called Opus Dei, 'has arisen in our day as a living expression of the perennial youth of the Church, ever open to the demands of a modern apostolate' (Paul VI). The Prelature proclaims that lay people can and ought to seek holiness in their ordinary life in the world. In response to a God-given call, members continue to work on their own initiative, while likewise seeking to be apostolic in all their normal surroundings. Since its founding on 2 October 1928, that has been Opus Dei's scope, the hallmark of its spirit. God's Work has welcomed and spiritually motivated people of every racial, social, and secular condition.

This book looks at the life of Opus Dei members, including their apostolic efforts, both personal and associated with others. It studies the Prelature's statutes and the writings, some hitherto unpublished, of its founder, Msgr Josemaría Escrivá. It opens with a short account of his life. (Unless otherwise indicated, all the quotations are from him.)

I have tried to identify the main features of Opus Dei and the kind of contribution it might be expected to make in building a more Christian world.

1

Msgr Josemaría Escrivá

INKLINGS

Childhood

The second of six children, Josemaría Escrivá de Balaguer y Albás was born on 9 January 1902, in the small north-eastern Spanish city of Barbastro. His father ran a retail business with two associates, selling chocolate and textiles. His mother, second youngest in a family of thirteen, had some French blood. Both parents gave their home an atmosphere of solid piety, devoid of show and intolerance; no less did they work at forming their children's character. The Escrivás weathered more than their share of setbacks: the death of their three youngest daughters in the space of just three years, the bankruptcy of Mr Escrivá's business, and a new start for the family in the unfamiliar city of Logroño.

Josemaría first crossed a school threshold at age three. During his teens, he became well read – far beyond high school requirements. He was especially keen on history and read many classical works of literature. Throughout his life, he could, with ease, quote Spanish and other authors.

Divine hints

Late December 1917: when he was about to turn sixteen, a small incident made a strong impression on Josemaría. Snow had fallen in Logroño. Making his way along his usual route, young Escrivá came across the freshly-made prints of a Carmelite monk's bare feet. A restlessness surged in his heart.

He began to sense that God was expecting something particular of him, although he didn't know precisely what. He later described these emotions as 'the first inklings of Love'. He resolved to attend Mass and receive communion daily, to intensify both prayer and penance. Hundreds of times a day he called on God with the prayer of the blind man of Jericho: Domine, ut videam! – Lord, that I may see!

Priesthood

He gave up the idea of becoming an architect and decided to study for the priesthood. He hoped that this step would make it easier for him to fulfil God's will, whatever specific turns it might take. In 1918, he began his priestly studies in the seminary of Logroño. Two years later, he moved to Saragossa to complete them. There, among other things, he attracted the attention of Cardinal Soldevilla. Saragossa's archbishop made him a supervisor for a year or two in the seminary. Still seeking to see his way more clearly, he spent many long nights in prayer.

While finishing his theological studies, Josemaría also began to study civil law, especially when the seminary was not in session. He was ordained a priest on 28 March 1925. Four months earlier, his father had died, worn out at fifty-seven.

A temporary assignment landed the new priest in a poor country parish. Two months later, he was back in Saragossa. His pastoral duties included teaching catechism in some slum neighbourhoods, visiting poor families, looking after a church, and helping his brothers in the priesthood. He continued to work toward his law degree. His fellow law students also met with his spiritual encouragement. He tutored in several areas of law. The income helped him support the family left in his charge: his mother, an older sister, and a little brother.

In March 1927, he obtained ecclesiastical permission to study for a doctorate in civil law in Madrid. There his studies competed with his priestly zeal: criss-crossing the city, bringing his ministry and smile to the hospitalised, to poor, abandoned children .... Every year he prepared thousands of them for first confession and Communion. He was appointed chaplain of the Foundation for the Sick, a charitable work for the destitute. He again took up tutoring. His days were long, tiring. He found strength in prayer and a tender devotion to the Blessed Virgin. His body met with rigorous penances. With all this he hoped that God would show him what direction he should take.

FOUNDATIONS

Opus Dei is born

During a retreat, on 2 October 1928, Josemaría saw (the only term he ever used) what God was expecting of him. God asked him to devote all his life to accomplishing what was later called Opus Dei. Henceforth, his mission was to urge men in all walks of life to respond to a specific vocation to be saints and apostles in the thick of the world. For them, there was to be no change of job, duties, or status – just a change of heart, to be reflected in that job, duties, status. (He also saw that to be able to reach everyone, he was to start with university people.)

From then on, Father Escrivá knew no 'tranquillity'. He added his new task to all the others. Penniless, his resources consisted of his 'twenty-six years of age, God's grace, and good humour'. Once more he went in search of strength among 'the incurably sick; the poor castaways; the homeless, unschooled children ... in hovels where despair had shrivelled the human heart ....' In those early years, he tended to thousands of people whose souls resembled their bodies. He wrote letters upon letters to friends, including fellow priests, in search of prayers, penance, and souls who could join him.

On 14 February 1930, a new inspiration from God made it clear that he was to spread the prospect of holiness in the world to women as well. Just a few weeks before, he had written, 'There will never be women in Opus Dei – not even in jest'. From then on, Opus Dei would have women as well as men as members, united by the same spirit.

At first, Father Escrivá's 'apostolic work' did not even have a name. One day, a friend asked him: 'How is that work of God coming along?' Something clicked; there was the name: the work of God, *Opus Dei, operatio Dei,* God's work; ordinary work made prayer along all the paths of the world.

How it grew

The founder sought souls wherever he could: in hospitals, churches, offices, classrooms .... There were a few vocations, although souls also slipped through his fingers 'like eels'. Near the end of 1933, he opened Academy DYA (initials in Spanish for 'Law and Architecture'), Opus Dei's first collective undertaking or 'corporate apostolate'. Financial straits did not clip Father Josemaría's apostolic wings. The following year, the Academy moved to roomier quarters, enough in any case to house a handful of college students. The academy-residence was left in shambles by the Spanish Civil War. One of its first incidents in Madrid took place across the street at a barrack.

Religious persecution unleashed during the conflict forced the founder into hiding here and there. Eventually in March 1937, he found a more secure refuge in the Honduras consulate. But his concern for souls in time led him to abandon the consulate at no little risk.

The first members of the Work finally convinced him to leave the Republican zone. In November 1937, accompanied by a few of them, he made a treacherous crossing of the Pyrenees: on foot, ill-clad, with hunger to match the cold.

The trek lasted two weeks and put them in Andorra; from there they re-entered Spain, via Lourdes. The first thing Father Escrivá did on reaching Spain was to make a retreat. Then, in and from the city of Burgos, he resumed his apostolic work. As best he could, he tried to make contact with all the persons he had known before the war.

As soon as the strife ended, he moved back to Madrid. Five months later, he had already set up a new student residence. Still Opus Dei's only priest, he tended to the new vocations, the residents – and the friends of both. He also served as chaplain at St Elizabeth's, both a church and a convent of enclosed Augustinian nuns. He confessed and spiritually guided hundreds of persons, men and women, single and married, students, professors, writers, artists .... He organised retreats and courses on spiritual development, ever pushing Opus Dei's expansion. On Saturday evenings, he would travel by train to various cities (Valencia, Barcelona, Saragossa, Valladolid), returning to Madrid by a late night train on Sunday. At the request of many bishops, he gave retreats to diocesan priests (during one of them he learned of the unexpected death of his mother). He also preached retreats to many religious communities, both men and women.

This intense activity in the 1940s took place against a background of calumnies and denunciations from a number of priests who, supposedly in good faith, regarded him as unorthodox – heretical in some cases – for advancing a calling to holiness 'on Main Street'. However, Madrid's bishop, conversant with Opus Dei's spirit, aims, and methods, did everything possible to shield the new group. From the start, he had encouraged Father Escrivá and blessed his work. On 25 June 1944, the bishop ordained the first three members of Opus Dei to become priests.

For some time, the founder had been wrestling with how Opus Dei might have its own priests. During Mass on 14 February 1943, the solution came to him: lay members would have to be trained and ordained. Since they would be schooled in the same lay spirit, they could form the new vocations, making it easier for the Work to expand. They would also help ensure that Opus Dei's pristine spirit was preserved and lived. Thus was born the Priestly Society of the Holy Cross. It represented a new *pastoral* phenomenon in the Church: men with university degrees and professional experience 'who, without expecting anything in return, give themselves to serve all souls, especially their brothers'. It was also something of a new *juridical* development: becoming an Opus Dei priest would not substantially modify the Christian vocation they, as laymen, had already committed themselves to live in all its fullness.

Crossing boundaries

The Spanish Civil War, and then World War II, kept Opus Dei from spreading beyond Spain. As early as 1935, Father Escrivá had dreamt of sending a member or two to Paris. When the World War ended, members of Opus Dei began to spread themselves to many countries: Portugal (1945), England and Italy (1946), France and Ireland (1947), the United States and Mexico (1949), Chile and Argentina (1950), Columbia and Venezuela (1951), Germany (1952), Peru and Guatemala (1953), Uruguay and Switzerland (1956), Brazil, Austria, and Canada (1957), El Salvador, Kenya, and Japan (1958), Costa Rica (1959), Holland (1960), Paraguay (1962), Australia (1963), the Philippines (1964), Nigeria and Belgium (1965), Puerto Rico (1969), and so on.

The founder closely followed the beginnings in each country. Often, the pioneers' 'sendoff' consisted of a blessing and an image of the Blessed Virgin – all Father Josemaría could spare. They would have to manage as best they could, counting, of course, on God's help. Whenever possible, the founder journeyed to points throughout Europe to prepare the ground and encourage those who were setting down roots.

At the end of 1946, the founder moved to Rome to be at

the heart of Christianity, close to Christ's Vicar and thereby to emphasise Opus Dei's universal scope. In 1948, he opened the Roman College of the Holy Cross, where male members would be educated and trained. In 1953, he did the same for women with the Roman College of St Mary. The expansion was paying off.

From Rome, Monsignor Escrivá (named a domestic prelate of the Pope in 1947) spurred and guided the myriad apostolic activities his sons and daughters had spawned. In directing Opus Dei, he was helped by two councils, one for men and the other for women. At the Work's headquarters, he also received the many people who came to see him and seek his counsel: Catholics, Christians of other denominations, Jews, agnostics .... He also accepted assignments from the Pope: member of the Pontifical Academy of Theology (1957), consultor to the Sacred Congregation for Seminaries (1957) and to the Pontifical Commission for Interpretation of the Code of Canon Law (1961).

Last years

The founder suffered greatly on account of the doctrinal confusion following the Second Vatican Council. In a spirit of reparation, he undertook penitential pilgrimages to various Marian shrines, including Our Lady of Pilar and that of Torreciudad (Spain), Fatima, Guadalupe, Loretto, Lourdes, Aparecida (Brazil), Lujan (Argentina), and so forth. On these occasions, he also met with many groups of people, some as large as several thousand. He always called these friendly, unpretentious gatherings catechetical, for he spoke winningly about God to people concerned about family life, apostolate, the meaning of suffering, education, and so forth. 1970 saw him visit Mexico. For two months in 1972, he crisscrossed the Iberian peninsula where he met with over 150,000 Spaniards and Portuguese. From May to August 1974, we find him in six South American countries; early in 1975, he visits Venezuela and Guatemala. More than a million people in Latin America were, thus, able to meet him.

On 28 March 1975, Monsignor Escrivá marked the golden anniversary of his ordination. It was all very private and quiet in keeping with his usual norm of conduct. 'My role is to hide and disappear, so that Jesus alone may shine'. (His travels in the 1970s had been a parenthesis in a quiet life dedicated to his priestly ministry and directing Opus Dei.)

In May 1975, he visited the shrine of Our Lady of Torreciudad (in northern Spain) – an ancient site for pilgrimages that he had transformed into a beautiful house of prayer to thank the Blessed Virgin. Since the beginning of the year, he took up again the plea of Bartimeus ('Lord, that I may see'), the very prayer with which he had stormed heaven during the decade before his vocation was made clear. Now, his desire was to see God face to face.

In Rome on 26 June 1975, upon entering the room where he had worked, he suddenly died.

A day in his life

As soon as Monsignor Escrivá got up, he would kiss the floor, saying *Serviam:* 'I will serve', thus offering to God the day that lay ahead. Then he would recite some prayers his mother taught him. There followed half an hour of mental prayer in preparation for Mass. He said the Mass with very great devotion, following which he recollected himself in thanksgiving to God. After breakfast, he would recite the breviary. Then followed office work and correspondence. At morning's end, he usually received visitors. At midday, he recited the Angelus; before lunch, a brief visit to the chapel. Every day, he read from the New Testament and from some spiritual classic. He also eked out time to review theology and do some general reading.

Monsignor Escrivá ate frugally, though when he had guests he kept his austerity to himself. Sometimes, alone, he would skip lunch. He would again make a short visit to the

Blessed Sacrament. After meals, he would spend half an hour conversing with a handful of his sons and then back to work. Daily, he prayed the three parts of the rosary, conveniently spread throughout the day. Late in the afternoon, he would devote another half hour to mental prayer, at a fixed time.

When the evening get-together ended, he would retire in silence to examine his conscience and say some last prayers. He prayed himself to sleep: spiritual communions, short vocal prayers ....

The man

So many testimonies and documents covering the founder's life give us an insight into what kind of man he was. People outside Opus Dei saw an intelligent, well-educated, vigorous man. His teachings and writings betray a legal background, both civil and ecclesiastical. His capacity for understanding and solving problems, his knowledge of men and things ran deep. His had also an uncommon foresight.

The Jewish psychiatrist, Victor E. Frankl, says he was fascinated by 'the refreshing serenity emanating from him and sparking our conversation ... also by the uncommon rhythm and flow of his thoughts; finally, his astonishing ability to establish immediate rapport with those at hand': whether one person or a vast audience, intellectuals or not, children or adults, old world Europeans or new world natives ....

His affection went out to all, even to those opposed to the Church or the Work. Everyone came away from his presence with the impression that he had nothing better to do than to be with them. Decades later, he could recall the tiniest details about people: their names, relatives, family affairs, and so on. His joviality and friendliness were infectious; everyone loved his company. If someone got sick, at his bedside would be found Monsignor Escrivá, cheering him up, helping him to pray. He quickly put visitors at ease, even when he was sick or had spent a sleepless night.

When he had to reprimand someone, he was clarity itself. But he suffered more than the person corrected. And invariably, then or later, would come the kind, gentle touch that helped the scolding be accepted but without extenuating it.

He gave no importance to his own person and deflected to God any compliments that came his way. His capacity for work and a knack for order led him to use his time extraordinarily well. He would pursue each task to the last detail, not taking on another until he had finished what was in hand. His writings display an open spirit, a sweep of literature and history, and a keen artistic taste.

This incomplete portrayal cannot end without my mentioning his *instinct* for the supernatural. Monsignor Escrivá loved God and the Church; that was so evident above all else. He was also a magnet for drawing souls to God. In a letter which Madrid's bishop sent in the 1940s to a Benedictine abbot near Barcelona to quell a calumnious campaign unleashed against Opus Dei's founder, we read: '... Escrivá is a model priest; chosen by God for the sanctification of many souls; humble, prudent, abnegated, extremely obedient to his bishop; remarkably intelligent with a very solid doctrinal and spiritual background; fervently zealous; an apostle for the evangelisation of youth'.

CONTINUITY

His successor

When Monsignor Escrivá died, Opus Dei had spread to five continents and comprised some 60,000 members of 80 nationalities. Observers have been struck by the fact that the founder's sudden death caused barely a ripple. This continuity speaks well of the members' faithfulness to the Work's spirit and the founder's legacy. Three months after his death, representatives from throughout the world gathered in Rome to choose his successor. Unanimously elected on the first ballot was Father Alvaro del Portillo, who for forty years had been Monsignor Escrivá's closest collaborator. When Opus Dei was made a personal Prelature in November 1982, Pope John Paul II appointed him as its first Prelate.

On 6 January 1991, Monsignor del Portillo was ordained bishop in St Peter's Basilica, Rome. The episcopal ordination of the Prelate of Opus Dei does not change in any way the nature of the Prelature, nor its relationships with the bishops of the dioceses where it carries out its apostolates.

Born in Madrid on 11 March 1914, Bishop del Portillo earned his first degree in civil engineering, later doctorates in history and canon law. Joining Opus Dei in 1935, he was one of the first three members ordained in 1944.

In addition to his priestly work and duties as Opus Dei's Secretary General, Bishop del Portillo played an active role in the Second Vatican Council, notably as president of the preparatory Commission for the Laity and as secretary to the Commission for the Discipline of the Clergy. He still acts as consultor to various congregations of the Roman Curia. As a papal nominee he attended the 1987 synod of bishops on the vocation of the laity in the Church and in the world, and the 1990 synod on the formation of priests. He also serves as chancellor of the Universities of Navarre (Spain), Piura (Peru), and La Sabana (Colombia). Two of his books have been published in English: *Faithful and Laity in the Church* (Ecclesia Press, Shannon 1972) and *On Priesthood* (Scepter, New York 1974).

The Work expands

After the founder's death, the Work continued to spread to nine nations and within those countries where it has made its home. What happens seems to be the same everywhere: some lay members of the Work find jobs in a new place and try to make lots of friends among colleagues, chance acquaintances, students. They offer them some traditional classes in Christian living. Vocations crop up ... a nucleus of new members is formed. An Opus Dei priest visits periodically to tend to them with, of course, the permission of the local bishop. Soon, it becomes necessary to find temporary premises; eventually an established centre of the Prelature is set up. In doing so, those who form the new outpost merely heed the founder's advice: 'You need to spread out the world over, in all the honest occupations of mankind, each of you attracting ten or so friends who in turn will draw others ... You must fan out'.

The number of vocations continues to grow. In 1988, a little over a decade after the founder's death, Opus Dei had more than 75,000 members of 87 nationalities. Since 1975, apostolic work has been going on in Bolivia, Honduras, Trinidad, Ivory Coast, Zaire, Hong Kong, Singapore, Cameroon, Macao, Sweden, Finland, Taiwan, Dominican Republic, Korea, New Zealand, Poland, Czechoslovakia, Hungary, and Yugoslavia.

Its founder saw God's Work continuing 'for as long as there are men on earth. No matter how much production methods may change, there will always be work that men can offer up to God and sanctify in his presence'. Since work is not about to disappear, that's one reason more why Opus Dei should not become outdated. Indeed, Monsignor Escrivá used to say: 'Ours is not an organisation that answers to a particular set of circumstances; we have not come to meet the needs of a specific nation or historical age. From the start, Jesus endowed his work with a universal, catholic heart'.

Opus Dei in Ireland

In Ireland, members are to be found all over the country, from Donegal to Cork, from Galway to Dublin. Most live in areas where centres of the Prelature have been set up:

Dublin, Galway, Tuam, Meath, and Limerick.

One of the first apostolic initiatives of members in Ireland was the establishment of Nullamore University Residence in Dartry, Dublin. The official opening in 1954 was attended by the Taoiseach, Mr John A Costello; the Chancellor of the National University of Ireland and leader of Fianna Fáil, Mr Eamon de Valera; the President of University College Dublin, Professor Michael Tierney, and the Registrar, Professor Jeremiah Hogan; the Lord Mayor of Dublin, Mr Alfie Byrne; and the Archbishop of Dublin, Dr John Charles McQuaid. Later years saw the expansion of Nullamore, which now houses 60 students from Ireland and abroad.

Further halls of residence were set up in the years that followed: Gort Ard (Salthill, Galway) in 1958; Glenard (Clonskeagh, Dublin) in 1962; Ros Geal (University Road, Galway) in 1972. Activities for students in Dublin are also held in study centres such as Cleraun (Mount Merrion), Carraigburn (Donnybrook) and Ely (Hume Street).

Over the years members have also set up a variety of youth clubs. These include the Helm Club (Galway), the Harrow Canoe Club (Ranelagh, Dublin), Dunevin (Synge Street, Dublin), Glenbeag (Clonskeagh), Nullamore Junior Club (Dartry, Dublin). The Anchor Youth Club in Artane on Dublin's northside started in 1966, and had its new premises opened officially by the Taoiseach, Mr Charles Haughey, TD, on 8 July 1989. These clubs offer a wide range of activities for young people.

Catering and educational centres such as Crannton (Dartry, Dublin) and Ballabbert (Tuam) and Lisdara (Navan) offer a two year course in catering and household administration leading to a City and Guilds qualification.

A variety of courses, including retreats, for members and others, are organised regularly throughout the year in two conference centres: Lismullin, at Tara, Co. Meath and Ballyglunin, near Tuam, Co. Galway.

In Ireland as elsewhere, the apostolic activity of members can be found in all sectors of society: among blue and white collar workers, academics and tradesmen, those working inside and outside the home, the unemployed, and among the young and old.

Opus Dei's information office is at 10 Hume Street, Dublin 2. Its headquarters are at Harvieston, Cunningham Road, Dalkey, Co. Dublin. Currently serving as Opus Dei's vicar for Ireland is Father Donal Ó Cuilleanáin, who before ordination worked as a mechanical engineer with Aer Lingus.

And in Britain

As in Ireland, members of the Work live in all parts of the country, but mainly in places where centres have been set up, with the previous agreement of the Ordinary of the diocese: Glasgow, Manchester, London (where the Work has developed most, with some 12 centres), and Oxford. Activities are also organised in Canterbury, Mansfield, Portsmouth, Southend, in mid-Sussex, and on Merseyside, although permanent centres have not yet been established in these places.

Some corporate apostolic activities have been started, such as Netherhall House, an international student residence in London; Lakefield Catering and Educational Centre, also in London, a school for training girls of school-leaving age in domestic and catering skills; and various residences for university students and clubs for young people around the country. These centres not only reach out to academic environments, but also extend to non-intellectual spheres, attracting employers as well as employees, appealing to the young as well as to older people.

Opus Dei's information office is at 5 Orme Court, London W2 4RL. Currently serving as vicar for Britain is Father Philip Sherrington.

United States: to & fro

In 1949, Father Joseph Muzquiz, one of Opus Dei's first three priests, and two lay members of Opus Dei arrived in the United States. The first US 'centre' of Opus Dei was a small hotel room in Chicago. The trio's dominion of English was a perfect match for their billfolds. But what a lot of praying ... and meeting people – not only in Chicago. The first American Opus Dei members often wondered which logged more miles: Father Joseph or his letters. But let's not get ahead of ourselves. Before 1949 was out, those pioneers purchased 'without any money' what was soon dubbed Woodlawn Residence, a roomy building next to the University of Chicago. A decade later, bigger or smaller centres dotted the Midwest (Milwaukee, Madison, St Louis, South Bend) and the East (Boston, Washington).

Sal Ferigle is now Father Ferigle, a priest of the Opus Dei Prelature, working as a chaplain for a student residence for college women near Boston University. Father Muzquiz died a few years ago while teaching a theology course to a group of women members attending a workshop at Arnold Hall, an Opus Dei conference centre near Cape Cod. Their work has been fruitful. The seed they came to sow in American soil has spread to the four corners of the country. Centres have been added from Los Angeles and San Francisco to New York, Providence and Delray Beach in Florida, as well as Pittsburgh and Houston. There are two conference centres where Opus Dei conducts retreats and workshops, the one near Cape Cod in Pembroke, Massachusetts, and another in Valparaiso, Indiana. Opus Dei members organise classes on doctrinal topics and on spiritual life at college campuses throughout the country: Carnegie-Mellon, Harvard, Maryland, Notre Dame, Pittsburgh, Princeton, Stanford, Wisconsin and many others.

Information on Opus Dei can be found in the *National Catholic Directory*, pertinent diocesan directories, and such national yearbooks as those for associations and non-profit groups. Articles on Opus Dei are found in all major encyclopaedias, including the *New Catholic Encyclopedia*. Opus Dei's information office is located at 330 Riverside Drive, New York, NY 10025. Its headquarters are found at 99 Overlook Circle, New Rochelle, NY 10804. Currently serving as Opus Dei's vicar for the US is Father James Kelly, who before obtaining in Rome an ecclesiastical doctorate earned an A.B. degree at Harvard and a doctorate in philosophy from the City University of New York.

As Opus Dei took root in the US, that growth soon benefited other parts of the globe. The first Filipinos, the first Australian, the first Canadian all met and joined Opus Dei while studying in the US. Moreover, American members have gone abroad to help in launching and sustaining apostolic work in Australia, the Philippines, Japan, Canada, Kenya, and Nigeria.

Whether in Nairobi or Los Angeles, friendship with a lay member of Opus Dei – usually a colleague or fellow student – is what often sets the spiritual ball rolling. For those who wish to explore or deepen their Christian life, Opus Dei offers a variety of spiritual means: personal spiritual guidance with one of its priests; practical courses in Christian living for small, homogeneous groups; days (or evenings) of recollection; retreats; visits to the poor or ill; teaching catechism in local parishes; conferences or lectures, and so on. Pope John Paul II, in a comment to the Opus Dei Prelate, observed that members have a 'charism' for getting people to sacramental confession. Above all, as Opus Dei's founder insisted, 'Unless you make them souls of prayer, you've wasted time: theirs and yours'.

A saint?

Even in life Monsignor Josemaría Escrivá had a reputation for holiness, which might be summed up in a private comment made by Paul VI. The Pope, who had known the founder since 1946, considered him to be 'in the Church's history the person who received the most charisms and responded to those gifts with the greatest generosity'.

That reputation for holiness, 'vouched by many authorised witnesses,' has grown since 26 June 1975, 'with significant spontaneity'. So wrote Cardinal Poletti in the decree that opened in Rome the process of beatification of Msgr Escrivá, less than six years after his death in 'the odour of sanctity'. Many thousands of letters asking that the process be opened had reached the Pope. They came from heads of state as well as peasants, public figures and entire families, people and institutions of every type from the four corners of the globe. Among them were petitions from 69 cardinals and 1,300 bishops (more than a third of the worldwide hierarchy), a unique fact in the annals of the Catholic Church.

On 9 April 1990, the Holy See published a decree of the Congregation for the Causes of Saints, in which Pope John Paul II declared that the Servant of God Josemaría Escrivá practised all the Christian virtues to an heroic degree. The founder of Opus Dei was therefore declared 'Venerable'. On 6 July 1991, a cure attributable to his intercession was formally declared to be miraculous by the Holy See. A Carmelite nun, on the point of death with several complaints and many tumours, some very large, was completely and permanently cured overnight. This formal recognition of a miracle by the Holy See is the final requirement before beatification.

Favours attributed to the Servant of God continue to reach the Roman office of his cause of beatification. Some are from countries where Opus Dei is not established, including many from behind the former Iron Curtain. They speak of material favours, among them inexplicable cures well supported by medical evidence. But the most common favours are of a spiritual kind, those that do not make headlines. A glimpse of these can be found in a periodic bulletin distributed free of charge by the pertinent national office of Opus Dei. (In the United States, write and ask for

Bulletin on the Life of Msgr Escrivá; 330 Riverside Drive; New York, NY 10025. In Ireland, the address is 22 Cunningham Road, Dalkey, Co. Dublin, and in Britain, 6 Orme Court, London W2 4RL). Opus Dei's founder (not for nothing does Escrivá in Spanish mean Scribe) is very much alive also through his published works. More than 6 million copies of his books are in print. (In the US his works are available from Scepter Press, 481 Main Street, New Rochelle, NY 10801. In Ireland contact Four Courts Press, Kill Lane, Blackrock, Co. Dublin, and in Britain, Scepter, 1 Leopold Road, London W5 3PB.)

Also under way are the processes of beatification of two members of Opus Dei: the Argentine engineer Isidoro Zorzano who died in 1943 and the young Spanish student Montserrat Grases who died in 1959 at the age of eighteen.

2

Original Spirituality

On 2 October 1928, the 26-year-old priest learned what God wanted of him. He saw God's Work clearly defined in all its ramifications. His insight was not a mere religious aspiration, but rather a very precise illumination, very clearly from God. This was 'no human undertaking, but a great supernatural enterprise. From the beginning, everything necessary for it to be called, without boasting, the "Work of God" has been fulfilled to the letter'.

At the very start, Father Escrivá was able to describe it all in detail to those he confided in. It seemed as if he were speaking of something long established. Yet in early writings, its novelty amazes even the founder. Everyone is called to intimacy with God and to share that friendship among one's peers, but without abandoning the world. Rather, those mundane realities, especially one's work, family burdens, and social duties are to be prayerfully converted into the service of God and others. The programme might seem viable now, but not so back in 1928. Its novelty can best be appreciated against the backdrop of the history of spirituality.

A call to seek God in the world, in one's occupation, makes no sense if one is not convinced that secular things can be sanctified and can sanctify the person engaged in them. But the whole perspective changes if one dwells long enough on the facts of creation and redemption: what came from God can be redirected to God in and through Christ. And that possibility becomes a reality, the founder urged, only if one commits himself or herself to sanctify them in answer to a divine calling to do that very thing. Monsignor Escrivá did not merely advance a theory of secular sanctification. Rather, he encouraged specific individuals to strive to be holy and apostolic right where lay men and women had always been. A truly pastoral phenomenon began to take shape 'fostered in our day by divine providence, for the good of the Church and all souls, with the abundant blessings of five popes' (Monsignor Carboni writing in *L'Osservatore Romano* when Opus Dei became a Prelature).

HISTORICAL BACKGROUND

From outside

During the first centuries of Christianity, work soon ceased to be seen as something good in itself and was mainly regarded as a simple ascetical means for combating sloth, the mother of all vices. So opined in any case St Athanasius and Cassian.

Meanwhile, cenobitic life (apart from the world and monastic in style) increasingly became the model. Among the more prominent Fathers of the Church, only St John Chrysostom (345–407) still paid any attention to work. In fact, he was the last to speak of sanctifying commonplace life until more than 1,500 years later when Vatican II took up the subject. After him, one gets the impression that the ordinary Christian was not called or expected to live the Gospel fully. Neither was the laity expected to be apostolic. Not even the individual hermit or monk. According to the Rule of St Benedict – the model constitution in the west for all subsequent religious communities – it is the monastery itself that is apostolic.

The appearance of mendicant orders in the thirteenth century brought a preached Christianity into public squares and marketplaces, as friars would leave the cloister to travel from town to town. This phenomenon does not point to the revaluation of ordinary work. Quite the reverse. While manual work performed in the monastery bore a certain material resemblance to work on the outside, the Dominicans and Franciscans failed to see and stress that discharging one's secular duties could be a veritable school of virtues. The polemics that then raged between mendicants and diocesan priests led the former to stress that it was even possible to achieve holiness without working. Instead, they would beg for alms to support themselves.

In effect, the theologians of the mendicant orders did not plumb the reality of work. They affirmed that manual work in the convent was not obligatory. Even St Thomas Aquinas considered secular occupations an obstacle to contemplation. St Bonaventure and many other theologians were of similar views.

Other mediaeval institutions more directly present in the workaday world, such as military orders and trade guilds, did not bring forth any ascetical or doctrinal teachings that would favour an awareness of the need or even possibility to direct work toward God.

In ensuing centuries, attention was deflected away from the duties that make up everyman's life. The author of *The Imitation of Christ* is even more negative toward the world than the desert Fathers. The latter at least saw work as a means to avoid the idleness that soon becomes the devil's workshop. St Ignatius in his *Spiritual Exercises,* largely followed the writing of the Spaniard Cisneros in this.

The Renaissance saw some positive developments. One has only to consider such men as St Thomas More and Erasmus. But the process was long and discontinuous. Luther's divorce from Rome in the sixteenth century, giving rise to Protestantism, postponed the discovery of the sanctifying value of work. Protestants believed original sin radically wounded human nature. Indeed their claim that human actions, even if inspired by grace, were devoid of any redemptive value was completely opposed to such a discovery.

The other great upheaval of the sixteenth century – the discovery of a new world awaiting evangelisation – might conceivably have favoured a development of a spirituality more in keeping with the needs of the time. But Catholic theology inspired in the Renaissance and Baroque allowed itself to be tainted by the aristocratic disdain for manual work and by a narrow, uninspiring moralism. The new theology was also suspicious of certain excesses, particularly in the area of mysticism. With Melchor Cano, it declared that lay people could not aspire to the peaks of Christian perfection.

Suarez, the distinguished Jesuit theologian, elaborated the theory of the *states*, according to which religious and bishops – and by analogy, priests – are by their vocation in a 'state of acquired perfection', which they then communicate to others. At best, ordinary faithful were to content themselves with crumbs fallen from this religious-clerical table. Subsequently, this theory rigidly constrained ways of thinking about the call to holiness.

In the seventeenth century, a reaction set in to acquaint ordinary Christians, at least some prominent ones, with the pathways of prayer. The most notable representative of this trend was Geneva's St Francis de Sales. Generally speaking, however, he went no further than to suggest that men and women in the world adopt – and adapt to their circumstances where necessary – means to sanctity followed in monasteries and convents. Since ordinary activities were still not seen as leading naturally or readily to union with God, spiritual writers too often put before butchers and bakers a secular-monastic hybrid that failed to do justice to either reality.

After the French Revolution, religious spirituality evolved towards greater presence in the world; more attention is paid to secular activities in general – not just to physical work. Nevertheless, the general attitude continues to view the world from the outside. Thus, the encouragement is to live 'like' the others, to 'go out' to or 'approach' the world, to 'unite' with those who work, and so on. The pious associations launched for the laity by clerics or religious of this time continued to locate the centre of spiritual life outside the world. Moreover, to the degree that these lay people were encouraged to be apostolic, their apostolate was seen as something external, as super-imposed on their presence in the world.

The net effect of these trends was that, at the time Opus Dei was born, many lay persons felt wrenched and as though torn between a desire for spiritual life (which seemed to imply a distancing from the world) and a desire to remain in the world, where they had built up their family, professional, and social life.

Usually, these pious souls embraced an ensemble of devotions and charitable works, trying to achieve 'as best they could' an echo of monks and nuns. The formula had serious shortcomings. First, the desire for holiness meant having to find periods for prayer *away from* one's usual occupations. Second, the goal of lay sanctity was still seen as necessarily inferior to that pursued by world-withdrawn religious. Third, by multiplying pious, virtuous, and charitable acts, the 'devout' lay person, steeped in this uneasy spirituality, will be tempted to turn his back on everyday duties. Wouldn't his work and duties of his state in life be seen as hindrances to his sanctification?

For others, the concept of lay spirituality took on an essentially moralistic character. The overriding concern became that of avoiding evil. One could thus pride oneself on being a good Christian by skirting sin in all its casuistical ramifications, especially those of the sixth commandment. But this concern with good behaviour ran the real risk of degenerating into little more than bourgeois respectability. At most, perhaps, the aim was to be a 'do-gooder'. But is the divine call for John and Jane Doe to be holy and apostolic to be reduced to that?

Opus Dei's advent

The religious orders and congregations had seen a development that brought them ever closer to a world bent on forgetting God. Then along came Opus Dei. Was it part of the trend to adapt an otherworldly spirituality to an increasingly pagan world? Or was it a new phenomenon? 'I consider the vocation of monks, nuns, religious sisters, and brothers to be necessary and beneficial to the Church', declared Monsignor Escrivá. 'But that path is not for me nor for the members of Opus Dei. It can be said that every member of Opus Dei came to the Work *on the explicit condition of not changing his or her state in life.*' [They remain in the 'secular' state, not changing to the 'religious' state.]

These two approaches to holiness move in opposite directions. The evolution of the religious state begins outside the world but draws ever closer to it, seeking an impact on it. The lay spirituality of Opus Dei, however, is born in and of the world; it seeks to make the temporal order holy from within, by leading it to God. It is addressed to ordinary men and women of all kinds who, while being in the world or, better said, being of the world (since they are ordinary lay people) aspire to be Christians from head to toe by reason of a divine vocation.

'Our vocation means that our secular condition, our ordinary work, our situation in the world, is our very path to God, to which we try to attract our peers. It is not a matter of using a secular job as a cover for our apostolic work. On the contrary, our occupation is the same one we would have had if we had not come to Opus Dei (the same we'd have if we were unfortunate enough to abandon our vocation). We are, my sons and daughters, ordinary people. When we work at matters of the world, we do so because that is our place, that is where we encounter Jesus Christ, where our vocation leaves us'.

This is what led Cardinal Luciani, the future Pope John Paul I, to write that, where St Francis de Sales proposed a spirituality *for* lay people, Monsignor Escrivá propounded a lay, secular spirituality. Its founder said that the pastoral phenomenon of Opus Dei 'does not arise in opposition to religious spirituality; it is a distinct outpouring of the perennial treasure of the Gospel'. It was born 'from below', from ordinary life, and 'is not a kind of compromise with the world, a "desacralisation" of the monastic or religious state. It is not the latest stage in the rapprochement of the religious to the world'.

Opus Dei's message is therefore something 'as old as the Gospel and like the Gospel, new'. It reaches back over the centuries to the first Christians, who normally lived and worked in the midst of society.

SANCTIFYING WORK

Basics

A text of the founder reveals the full scope of the kind of sanctification he preached: 'Anyone who thought that our supernatural life would be favoured by turning our back on work would not understand our vocation. For us in fact, work is a specific means to holiness. Our interior life – contemplatives on the streets – takes its origin and impulse from the external life of work of each of us. We cannot separate interior life from apostolic work: it is all one thing. External work should not interrupt our praying, just as the beating of our heart does not break or diminish attention to our activities, whatever they may be'.

Monsignor Escrivá puts in relief the implications of the passage of Genesis (2:15) that says that man has been created *ut operaretur:* 'to work'. If that is the human condition, then ordinary work is the very hinge of his sanctification and the right human and supernatural setting for helping his fellow men.

That this statement from Genesis about work comes before the fall of our first parents implies that work is of the very essence of the human condition. Only the laborious and tedious side of human activity is punishment for original sin. In itself work is something good, noble. Man attains his full self-realisation through work. Here too is manifested his superiority to other creatures.

Work in its broadest sense forms part of God's plan for man. It is 'a means whereby man becomes a participant in creation. Hence, work, any kind of work, is not only worthy, it is also a means for attaining both human (that is, earthly, natural) and supernatural development'.

Man is a co-creator as well as a co-redeemer with God. Christ was a worker. St Joseph taught him his carpenter's trade. Work, therefore, is something that has been redeemed. It is not just the raw material of human life; it is a road to holiness: something that both sanctifies and can be sanctified. For man-in-the-world, his occupation becomes the hinge on which turns the whole task of impregnating his life with charity.

This is what led Opus Dei's founder to sum up life on earth by saying that one must 'sanctify work, sanctify oneself in one's work, and sanctify others through one's work'. The three facets are interconnected: personal holiness ('sanctify oneself in one's work') and giving apostolic witness ('sanctify through work') are not goals that can be achieved by minimising or shortchanging work itself. Holiness and being apostolic are achieved *through working,* while this same work constitutes a central part of human existence and so itself needs to be sanctified.

Sanctifying work

The first element of that trio is the sanctification of work carried out in the world. The world in itself is good, for it comes from God's hands. The hatred, pride, violence, rivalries, and the like that infest work stem from Adam and Eve's original sin and the personal sins of all subsequent men and women. Sins are what corrupt the world and turn it away from God.

Opus Dei looks on the world with optimism: each Christian is entrusted with the mission of restoring it to its original goodness and leading it back to God. Then the world becomes an occasion of holiness. In contrast to the 'contempt for the world' or 'abandoning the world' that characterise the religious vocation, Monsignor Escrivá prompts us to love the world to such an extent that we transform it. 'Because it is the setting for our life, because it is our place of work, because it is our battlefield – a splendid battle of love and peace – and because it is where we must sanctify ourselves and our fellow men'. He saw the whole of creation as needing to be led back to God. Just as King Midas transformed all he touched into gold, human work needs to become 'through love, God's Work, Opus Dei, *operatio Dei*, a supernatural work'.

Once this principle is established, it follows that all noble occupations, especially work, are called to be manifestations of love and service. Insofar as work is a sharing in God's creative activity, the Christian must view work and all other human realities from God's perspective. No work or task is to be rejected. All employments are of value in God's service. All of them are of the greatest importance because, in the final analysis, their 'worth depends on the love of God we put into them'.

Monsignor Escrivá rebelled against any attempt to classify people according to their occupations, as if some jobs were better than others. As he stated, 'What does it matter to me if a member be a cabinet minister or a street sweeper? What I care about is that he grow in love for God and all men in and through his work'.

Such a concept of work allows one to aim at 'placing Christ at the peak of all human activities', that is, to lead them all to their fullness and draw from them all possible spiritual consequences. This implies two things for any Christian.

First, he ought to do his work as well as he possibly can, both humanly and supernaturally. For work to be thus divinised, it must be carried out with a supernaturally upright intention. Opus Dei's founder sums it up like this:

'Add a supernatural motive to your daily work, and you will have sanctified it'. One also sanctifies one's job by focusing faith's light on it and thereby discovering its ultimate purpose – the absolute good, God himself – and by learning to carry it out with charity and hope. This ultimate supernatural purpose forms part of the plan of redemption; it incorporates and sublimates all lesser aims (what man naturally pursues in keeping with creation), which both manifest and call forth God's grace. An 'essential part of sanctifying ordinary work, thus, consists in "working well, with human perfection also, and fulfilling as well all professional and social obligations'.

Secondly, a Christian is spurred to evaluate his environment in search of ways 'to restore the world to its due divine goodness'. He's also obliged to figure out ways to exert good influence on it according to the Church's social teachings. Through work, man leaves his stamp on creation. Work enables him to sustain his family, improve society, abet mankind's progress. And he does so by developing ways of life, fellowship, and fraternity that make society more human and so more open to welcoming God's good news.

Sanctifying oneself

The second aspect of the spirituality of work laid down by Monsignor Escrivá has to do with personal sanctification through work. 'What good is it to me if so-and-so is said to be a good son of mine, a good Christian, but a bad shoemaker! If he doesn't strive to learn his trade well or doesn't give it due attention, he won't be able to sanctify it or offer it to God. Doing one's ordinary occupation as well as possible is the hinge of true spirituality'.

Work shows itself to be a privileged arena where practically all virtues are called for and exercised. Indeed, work done in God's presence is continual prayer, since the theological virtues that are the peak of Christian life are brought into play, namely: faith, hope, and charity. Let's see their role in work.

Charity: This God-centred love is practised 'by striving to seal all one's deeds with love for God, generously serving one's fellow men, all souls'. The person who does his job conscientiously renders a direct service to society, lightens others' burdens, and helps provide assistance to less fortunate individuals and peoples. Mankind's problems cannot be solved by justice alone. Charity is also needed, as in the time of the apostles. They blazed a path in the corrupt pagan world of their day by means of this supernatural virtue. Charity is 'a generous overflow of justice'. And God has ordained that the first demand of justice is to do one's duty, with God's help. 'The way to start is by being just; the next step is to do what is charitable ....' To do this means working for others. God puts a choice before us: either to work for ourselves, selfishly, or to dedicate ourselves to serving others.

Faith is also present in work. On the one hand, Monsignor Escrivá is convinced that a person's normal occupation, however ordinary and commonplace it might seem, has great value in God's eyes, in the plan of salvation. On the other hand, for him, Christ's presence in the depths of the soul whets one's faith, constantly stimulating contemplation. 'Our life is to work and to pray and vice versa. For the moment comes when we can no longer distinguish between these two concepts. Contemplation and action end up meaning the same thing in our mind and soul'. If the ordinary Christian does not work, if he does not discharge his obligations, his prayer life is a sham. And where there is no contemplation, there is no point in pretending to work for Christ.

Hope comes into play: one hopes to be able to reach sanctity through one's work and to obtain from God the reward that this work deserves, for no sincere effort is in vain. One must also have *fortitude* to persevere day after day, however difficult things become, whatever the external circumstances, until the task is completed, overcoming setbacks and limited resources, always trying to give good example. One also needs *prudence:* the hindsight and foresight to see what one ought to do in each situation and how to set about doing it. Work also develops other social virtues such as loyalty, faithfulness to commitments and demands of friendship, resourcefulness, and the naturalness that avoids anything strange or unfitting to one's position. This naturalness is a sign of the human and spiritual maturity of a person who fully shoulders his responsibilities; it also shows his humility in not seeking personal satisfaction but God's will alone. ('When you hear the plaudits of triumph, let there also sound in your ears the laughter you provoke with your failures'.)

For Monsignor Escrivá, 'ordinary life is not without its value. If doing the same things day after day seems boring, dull, and monotonous, it can only mean that love is in short supply. When there is love, each new day has another colour, a different rhythm, a novel harmony.'

Holiness cannot, therefore, be reserved to a few privileged souls – those ordained to the priesthood or those whose religious calling sets them apart from the world. The message of Opus Dei's founder is much more optimistic and open. When it was first heard, it sounded revolutionary: all men and women of every race, culture, tongue, profession, and social condition can and should aspire to holiness. Sanctity is one and the same for all: it means progressive identification with God himself, in whose image and likeness man has been created. Each one must seek to be holy in his own personal circumstances. This is what, 35 years later, Vatican Council II declared.

Sanctifying others

The call to work in some profession or trade cannot be divorced from one's condition as a Christian. Rather, it should be the 'lamp that gives light' to colleagues and friends. Sanctifying temporal structures, in the founder's mind, is an apostolic dimension that cannot be dissociated from a Christian's relations with individuals.

Each person's occupation and social situation weaves a web of relations with colleagues, relatives, neighbours, fellow club members, etc. This is how family and social relationships are always built up. Sincere, true, disinterested friendship leads to the greatest good: God himself. A friendship based on sacrifice spontaneously brings about trust. A friend's heart is attentive to all of one's problems, desires, and feelings. 'Those words whispered at the proper time into the ear of your wavering friend; that helpful conversation you manage to start at the right moment; the ready advice that improves his studies; and the discreet indiscretion by which you open for him unsuspected horizons for his zeal – all of that is the "apostolate of friendship"'.

In the founder's words, Opus Dei is 'one big catechism'. By example and friendly doses of Christian teaching, members of Opus Dei seek to dispel ignorance, 'God's greatest enemy'. This teaching is, above all, carried out in the one-on-one encounters that arise between co-workers. Life offers many natural opportunities to talk about God, to bare one's soul, to describe the life each Christian should lead in the different situations that crop up in ordinary life. Speaking from experience, the founder would exhort his audience: 'Work at your job, trying to fulfil the duties of your state in life, doing your job, your everyday work, properly, improving at it, getting better each day. Be loyal; be understanding with others and demanding of yourself. Be mortified and cheerful. There you have your apostolic role. Then, though you won't see why (all you can see is your wretchedness), you'll find that people come to you. Then you can talk to them quite simply and naturally on your way home from work, for instance, or in a family gathering, in a bus, walking down the street, anywhere. You will chat about the longings we all feel deep in our souls, even though some may not want to notice them. They will come to understand them better and consequently they'll start to look for God in earnest'.

This is the service the Catholic Church expects from Opus Dei members. As we read in the solemn decree approving Opus Dei, *Primum Inter* (16 June 1950), it is a service offered 'through the example they give to their fellow citizens, their colleagues and workmates, in family, civil, and professional life, by striving always and everywhere to be the best'.

Work well done is always exemplary. A Christian must bring to it all the perfection he or she is capable of on the human natural level (professional competence) and on the divine level (for love of God and to serve souls). By objective standards, one's work must be seen to be well done. It is difficult for work to be sanctified unless the worker aims at perfection. Without that excellence, it would be almost impossible to earn the necessary prestige, described by Monsignor Escrivá as the 'podium from which you will teach others to sanctify their work and adapt their lives to the demands of Christian faith'. Hence the need for on-going professional training to acquire all the knowledge one can. To win over others, a person must take to heart his need to fulfil his duties as well as the best of his companions and, if possible, better than the best.

Obviously, then, apostolate is not just spreading some pious practices that distantly relate to what takes up the greater part of one's time. 'The apostolic concern that burns in the hearts of ordinary Christians' needs to be intimately bound up with everyday work. Sanctifying one's work should lead simultaneously to the friendship that wins others for God and to serving them and all society.

FREEDOM AND RESPONSIBILITY

Why freedom?

One of Opus Dei's traits, so often highlighted by its spokesmen and even more so by the founder, is love for freedom. Holding freedom in such high regard is closely linked to Opus Dei's inherently secular outlook. It means that in all professional, political, social, and similar matters, each member acts according to a well-formed conscience and accepts responsibility for all consequences of his decisions and actions. He or she learns not only to respect but positively to love and promote true pluralism, the variety of everything human. The Declaration of the Sacred Congregation for Bishops on 23 August 1982, says: 'As regards choice in professional, social, political matters and so on, the lay faithful belonging to the Prelature enjoy, within the limits of Catholic faith and morals and Church discipline, the same freedom as other Catholics, their fellow citizens; as a result, the Prelature is not responsible for the professional, social, political, or economic activities of any of its members'.

Opus Dei's commitment to freedom is not a matter of tactics or shrewdness. Rather, it is the logical consequence of Opus Dei members' awareness that they share in the one mission of the Church, the salvation of *all* souls.

It is true that the Christian spirit lays down certain general ethical principles for temporal action: respect and support of the Church's teaching authority; noble and loyal behaviour that fosters charity; understanding and respect for others' opinions; true love of one's country, free from narrow nationalism; promoting justice; readiness to make sacrifices in the interests of the civic community, and so forth. However, on the basis of these principles each Christian person can choose, from among the different possible solutions or options open to him, whatever he thinks best. Monsignor Escrivá states: 'With our blessed freedom, Opus Dei can never be, in the public life of a country, something like a political party. There is and always will be room within Opus Dei for all the outlooks and approaches allowed by a Christian conscience. It is furthermore prohibited that the directors should bring any influence to bear'. Only the hierarchy of the Church has the authority to establish a specific norm of behaviour for all Catholics, in the rare event that the Church's welfare should demand such a monolithic manoeuvre.

This programme of personal holiness and apostolate in ordinary life, especially in the professional world, cannot be successful without the freedom that is the birthright of men and women created in God's image. Freedom is essential to Christian life, especially when each person assumes full responsibility for his own affairs.

Christianity is of its nature a religion of freedom. This was patent to Opus Dei's founder. 'God wants us to serve him freely – where the Lord's spirit is, there is freedom (2 Cor 3:17) – and, therefore, any apostolic action that does not respect freedom of consciences would certainly be wrong'. Some people fear that promoting freedom could undermine the faith. That would indeed be the case if the freedom in question were an aimless freedom: lawless and irresponsible. Such freedom would really be licence – equivalent to thinking that anything pleasing, anything one felt like doing, was morally good even if it involved rejecting God. This may be the end-result of what is called 'freedom of conscience', not to be confused with 'freedom of consciences'. With Leo XIII, Monsignor Escrivá declared: 'I defend with all my strength the freedom of consciences, which means that no one may licitly prevent a person from worshipping God'. While man has a serious duty to search for truth, no one may compel him to practise a faith he has not received nor to profess it in a particular way where God leaves us free to choose.

Opus Dei attacked

The total respect for freedom as inculcated by Monsignor Escrivá from the very beginning of Opus Dei was not always well understood. Perhaps, Spain in the 1940s and 1950s was not ready for it, particularly in clerical circles. Certain spiritual trends of the time, born of various theological schools, ascetical approaches, and apostolic viewpoints had created deep divisions among the Spanish laity and gave rise to a certain 'messianic' tendency. Each little group claimed it had 'the solution' to all the world's problems. This is what Monsignor Escrivá called 'the pseudo-spiritual one-party mentality', with everyone thinking that his principles and attitudes are the only valid ones and consequently should be adopted by all. It is then only a short step – easily taken – to regarding others' views as pernicious or heretical.

Thus, the opposition that arose from 1929 on (see *Conversations with Monsignor Escrivá,* nos. 33, 64–66) can be explained by a misunderstanding of Opus Dei's basic message. Nobody believed it possible to strive for holiness in the world. The year 1939 saw an increase in criticism and persecution of Opus Dei by 'good people', who, as the forgiving founder said, 'did so much evil while perhaps thinking they were doing God a service'.

Some attacks were made in the confessional or from the pulpit. Others were served up by the press or by those good people in their visits to the families of Opus Dei members. No little anxiety was caused when parents were told that their children 'could go to hell', because they had been 'led to believe' that one could be holy in the world. Students were sent to spy on Opus Dei centres and to denounce the heresies and deviations that took place there. One day, Father Escrivá's first book, *The Way,* was publicly burned in a convent school in Barcelona, where the provincial governor had issued a warrant for the arrest of its author. The founder was also denounced before the special Tribunal for the Repression of Masonry (a post-Civil War institution). It was described as a 'Jewish branch of freemasonry' or 'a Jewish sect connected with freemasonry'. Later, Monsignor Escrivá was accused before the Holy Office, now the Congregation for the Doctrine of the Faith, after the Holy See had granted Opus Dei its definitive approval.

The founder suffered because of the obstacles placed in

the way, above all, because of the harm caused to souls, not least the souls of the 'good people' instigating the attacks. In spite of everything, he never lost his serenity; he was not even particularly surprised by this development. 'A picture that is all light and no shadow would not be a picture! ... So, misunderstandings and opposition serve a purpose'.

What lay behind the misunderstandings and even the campaigns against Opus Dei? Interestingly enough, they were born of a clash between two outlooks (one religious and the other secular) that should have complemented one another. From a few ecclesiastical corners, they spread to others usually hostile to the Church. They still crop up from time to time.

Freedom and work

The freedom of Opus Dei members is seen first of all in their everyday work. They freely choose their own line of work and then freely set about choosing the means wherewith to do it as well as they can. Members are accountable only to whoever is over them at work – for example, the owner of the company or the head of a government department. But they never answer to the Work's directors.

If Opus Dei does not interfere in their work, still less does it exploit members' professional clout to obtain privileges or preferences of any kind. Such a move would run counter not only to the spiritual nature of the institution but to the basic fair play expected of any honest person, Christian or not. Monsignor Escrivá put it pointedly: 'Opus Dei is an apostolic undertaking. Its only concern is with souls. Fortunately, our spirit does not permit us to behave like a mutual-help organisation'.

The only influence Opus Dei has on its members' work is through the spiritual coaching it gives them, which impels them to become increasingly aware of the Gospel's implications and to strive to be more faithful to it in their daily lives.

While God's Work tries to make members increasingly sensitive to questions of social justice, at the same time, it leaves the door open to a wide variety of solutions. For the founder, 'the Catholic solution' to many problems facing the world does not exist. Any solution will be Christian if it respects natural law and the Gospel. He, therefore, stressed not the material aspect of the solution but the spirit that should impregnate it.

With this emphasis, he energetically encouraged each individual to shoulder his responsibilities. It would be criminal to 'remain passive when confronted by all the injustice, social and personal, that the depraved human heart can cause'. Monsignor Escrivá denounced a situation so often found in society: 'So many centuries of people living side by side and still so much hatred, so much destruction, so much fanaticism stored up in eyes that refuse to see and in hearts that refuse to love! The good things of the earth monopolised by a handful of people ... the world's culture limited to cliques .... And everywhere a hunger for bread and education .... Human lives – holy, because they come from God – treated as mere things, as statistics at best ....'

A businessman, for example, motivated by this concern, will be opposed to unfair competition, fraud, or price hikes due only to a monopoly. Rather, he will favour honesty in commercial dealings; he will pay special attention to his employees' problems and living conditions. He will always try to be just in relations with his workers and so on. In turn, a Christian worker will strive to fulfil all his duties faithfully. Like-minded citizens will exercise their rights and shoulder their responsibilities with an eye to the good of others and the country.

The influence of Opus Dei's spirit on society is far from insignificant. But in the last analysis, it boils down to whatever personal influence individual members may acquire through their professional achievements and their standing in their particular occupation.

A desire to contribute to the solution of social problems

– and here a Christian has much to offer – leads some Opus Dei members to join with other citizens to bring about apostolic initiatives that have considerable social impact.

In reply to 'organised defamations,' Monsignor Escrivá said it would be absurd to think that Opus Dei as such could manage mines, banks, or any other commercial ventures. The founder realised that a partisan minority will refuse to understand the practical consequences of freedom. They 'would like us to explain things in their way – in terms of power struggle and pressure groups. When we don't, they continue to allege deception and sinister intrigue'.

Opus Dei members, of course, resent such insinuations. For them, it is unthinkable that they should use their membership in the Prelature for personal aims, professional advancement, or social climbing, as if Opus Dei were some sort of old boys' network. Neither can membership be used to impose one's opinion on others. The other members would simply not tolerate it. They would insist that the opportunist 'change his attitude or leave the Work. This is a point on which no one in Opus Dei will ever permit the slightest concession. It is their duty to defend not only their own personal freedom but also the supernatural character of the activity to which they have dedicated their lives. That is why I think that personal freedom and responsibility are the best guarantee of the supernatural purpose of God's Work'.

If some Opus Dei members occupy important positions or have high social standing, they do so, thanks to their own efforts to sanctify their work – never to pressure from Opus Dei or favouritism from other members.

Freedom and politics

Those who do not believe that religious ideals and moral values can unite politically diverse people in a common undertaking could well reflect on a sociological reality: Opus Dei members belong to 87 nationalities and all social classes, races, and cultures, throughout the six continents. Each of them lives with his own family and works in his pertinent environment. How could an institution impose on such heterogeneous and widely dispersed individuals a single political criterion, a dogma if you will, in an area as relative and debatable as politics? How could a Kenyan be asked to model his conduct on that of an Australian, a Guatemalan, a Filipino, a Singaporean, or that of someone from Luxembourg?

Indeed, Monsignor Escrivá repeatedly stressed that by its very nature, 'Opus Dei is not tied to any person, any group, any government, any political idea'. In an instruction drawn up for Opus Dei directors, he told them not to talk about politics and to show that in Opus Dei 'there is room for all opinions that respect the Church's rights'. He added that the best guarantee that directors will not interfere in matters of opinion is the members' awareness of their freedom. 'If directors were to impose a specific criterion in temporal affairs, the other members who thought differently would immediately rebel – and rightly so. I would see myself having the sad duty of blessing and praising those who firmly refused to obey, and of correcting with holy indignation directors who wished to exercise an authority they can never have'.

Moreover: 'A long time ago, I wrote that if Opus Dei had been involved in politics, even for an instant, in that moment of error I would have left Opus Dei. One can't give the slightest credit to a news item that mixes Opus Dei up in politics or economics or temporal affairs of any kind. On the one hand we operate in the light of day, always reflecting strictly spiritual aims. On the other hand, Opus Dei men and women enjoy, in all matters the Church leaves to their judgment, complete personal freedom, respected by all, and consequently they are fully and personally responsible. Therefore, it's impossible for Opus Dei to involve itself in activities not directly spiritual and apostolic'.

The pluralism found in Opus Dei poses no problems. As

early as 1930, the founder wrote that pluralism is 'a sign of good spirit, of the uprightness of our common action, and of respect for the legitimate freedom of each individual'. It is worth noting that in Spain, in particular circumstances long since passed, the presence of three members in a Franco cabinet gave rise to interpretations that seemed to ignore the fact that, at the same time, other Opus Dei members were in the vanguard of the opposition and sometimes were victimised by the arbitrariness of the same Franco government.

A journalist from *Le Monde* asked the founder in 1972 if one could speak of an Opus Dei 'conspiracy': 'Impartial observers think not. There would need to be some kind of ideology and there is none. The civic freedom its members enjoy seems to be the reason for its success'.

Respecting freedom

Opus Dei members who choose to take an active part in political life do so with complete freedom. They receive no instructions or recommendations of any kind. Opus Dei's only influence is on the same level here as in work generally – to remind them of the need to act in accordance with their faith. This should be seen 'in the care you take to practise the supreme commandment of charity, overcoming all human passion, in the thoughtfulness with which you express your points of view as you study issues, avoiding heated arguments; by your respect for complete freedom of opinion in all spheres of human activity; by the understanding – frankness – with which you treat those persons holding opposite views'.

This attitude of respect explains why you find in Opus Dei such a wide range of people. This variety also stems from the fact that Opus Dei's apostolate is not restricted to persons of a particular social condition or way of thinking: it reaches out to all men of good will who wish to avail themselves of its spiritual coaching. Those who approach the Prelature are drawn by the strength of a deep faith lived and undaunted by human obstacles. The majority of Prelature members 'in all countries are labourers, housewives, shop-keepers, clerks, and so on: that is, people whose jobs carry no special political or social weight'.

Respect for freedom in temporal affairs must also extend to matters that affect the faith and call upon Catholics to obey the Church. 'I don't understand the use of pressure either to persuade or to impose', the founder said in this context. 'A person who has received the faith always feels that *he* is the victor. Error is fought by prayer, by God's grace, by talking things over calmly, by study, and by getting others to study! And, above all, by charity'.

Other spheres of freedom

Research: Without labouring the point, I would like to refer to what the founder said about freedom in scientific research. In October 1967, he conferred honorary degrees at the University of Navarre on academics who included Jean Roche, rector of the Sorbonne. Monsignor Escrivá recalled the university's role to serve man and be a leaven in society. 'It must seek truth in all spheres, in theology just as in the humanities and the natural sciences ... and in other branches of learning'.

The attitude of a Christian scientist consists in pursuing research with an open mind and no shirking of effort. This is not always easy. In a similar ceremony in 1974, in honour of Prof. Jerome Lejeune of Paris and Bishop Hengsbach of Essen (Germany), Monsignor Escrivá declared that 'scientific objectivity rightly rejects all ideological neutrality, all ambig-uity, all conformity, all cowardice: love of truth absorbs the entire life and work of a man of science'. He must beg for divine assistance, aware that the discovery of new know-ledge is the fruit of God's will, who thus reveals himself progressively to men.

To be truly scientific, all research must necessarily lead to God. The founder did not mean by this that theology should invade the realm of academic research. On the contrary, he denounced any claims that would reduce the autonomy of scientific inquiry. This was a logical result of his love for personal freedom, for autonomy in temporal affairs, and for the rights of people to go about their work – in this case their search for truth – in an upright way.

Monsignor Escrivá defended 'the personal freedom of every layman to take, in the light of Church-taught principles, all the decisions, theoretical and practical, he considers most appropriate and most in line with his own personal convictions and aptitudes. These would include, for instance, decisions regarding different philosophical or political theories, different artistic or cultural trends, or the problems of professional and social life'.

Theology: In the more restricted sphere of theology, Opus Dei members can freely contribute to the doctrinal apostolate by means of their research and speculation. They can enrich the treasury of wisdom with new knowledge and suggest new solutions for new problems as well as old. They accept in advance that they must submit to the higher judgment of the Church and stay within the limits of her teaching. They have exactly the same freedom as all other Catholics to form their own opinions in philosophy, theology, scripture, canon law, and the like. They can have disciples, but they cannot form a school to which the other Opus Dei members are obliged to belong. The creativity and freedom of choice of each member is fully respected.

This being said, all the Prelature's faithful respect the general law of the Church forbidding books harmful to faith and morals. Whenever for good reasons, such as, say, research for a dissertation, they must read such books, they are quite happy to seek advice beforehand and later to write critical articles by which others benefit from their opinions and analysis.

Monsignor Escrivá often commented that Opus Dei's fully secular spirit and approach gives its members a special facility to seek truth in freedom. That very freedom, united to charity, leads them to desire and defend the personal freedom of all men.

What I have said about freedom would be incomplete if I did not make one further point. When asked about the 'liberation' the world craves for, the founder replied without the slightest hesitation: 'Free yourself from sin. Free yourself from the chains of your evil passions. Free yourself from vice. Free yourself from bad company. Free yourself from indifference. Free yourself from disfigurement of soul and body'. He himself fostered many initiatives in favour of the underprivileged, but this did not prevent him from saying that 'to want to free oneself from pain, from poverty, from wretchedness is splendid, but it is not liberation. Liberation is the opposite. Liberation is ... to accept suffering with joy, to accept illness gladly, to accept a stifling cough with a smile!'

Personal responsibility

Underlying this affirmation of freedom, we always find in the founder's teachings the other side of the coin: personal responsibility. Freedom and responsibility are equally important, he argued. They are like 'two parallel lines'. Without freedom there can be no responsibility, and without responsibility there is no freedom. Now that so many try to shrug off the consequences of their deliberate acts, Opus Dei members must be ready to take full responsibility for their own actions, and all that follows from them, since 'nobody can make our choices for us'.

For the founder, it was intolerable that any member of the Prelature (or other Christians, for that matter) should implicate Opus Dei or the Church – or even worse claim to act in their name – when merely expressing personal views. Legitimate though they be, opinions can never be put forward as dogmas.

VATICAN II AND OPUS DEI

The discerning reader will have noted that the aspects of Opus Dei's spirituality described here are very reminiscent of certain texts of the Second Vatican Council. I refer particularly to Chapters IV and V of the dogmatic constitution, *Lumen Gentium*, which deal with the laity and the universal call to holiness; the decree, *Apostolicam Actuositatem*, on the apostolate of lay people; the dogmatic constitution, *Gaudium et Spes*, regarding the Christian's freedom and responsibility and the holiness of matrimony; the decree, *Presbyterorum Ordinis*, on the priesthood and holiness, etc.

The Council said, for example, 'It is quite clear that all Christians in any state or walk of life are called to the fullness of Christian life and to the perfection of love'. The laity have as their vocation 'to seek the kingdom of God by engaging in temporal affairs and directing them according to God's will'. Seeing in their daily work an 'extension of the Creator's work', they contribute to the redemption of the whole world and to the achievement of a 'higher sanctity, truly apostolic'. Indeed 'the Christian vocation is, of its nature, a vocation to the apostolate ... to be a leaven in the world'. Lay people 'strive to carry out their family, social and professional duties with such Christian generosity that their behaviour gradually permeates their environment and their work'.

These brief quotations from the Council – there are many more – echo the spirituality Monsignor Escrivá proposed since 1928. 'This is why he has been unanimously acknowledged as a precursor of the Council' (Cardinal Poletti, in the decree opening the founder's cause of beatification). Similarly he was called 'a pioneer of lay spirituality, opening up the path to holiness for men and women of all social conditions, anticipating, with the intuition of a holy instrument of God, the declarations that we read in the documents of Vatican II on the mission of the laity in the Church' (Cardinal Casariego of Guatemala in a homily at the

54

ordination of 54 members of Opus Dei).

In his memoirs, Cardinal Frings refers to the criticism initially made of Opus Dei's founder and to the joy he felt on seeing the Council 'take up his ideas and openly proclaim them'. Cardinal Baggio states that 'many thought it a heresy [to proclaim that sanctity was not the preserve of a privileged few] ... but since Vatican II, this proposition has become self-evident. However, what continues to be revolutionary in the spiritual legacy of Monsignor Escrivá is the *practical manner* of guiding men and women, whatever their condition, the "man in the street", towards sanctity ... This is why,' adds the Cardinal, 'the life, work, and message of Monsignor Escrivá constitute a turning point, or rather a new unpublished chapter, in Christian spirituality'. Wrote Cardinal Koenig: 'When he founded Opus Dei in 1928, Monsignor Escrivá already anticipated much of what has become, with Vatican II, the common patrimony of the Church'.

Many other Council fathers recognised Opus Dei's close link to its documents. This recognition was to be extended in the subsequent establishment of the Work as a personal Prelature. Finally, in this connection, let me quote something John Paul II said to some Opus Dei members when he celebrated Mass for them in 1979: 'Your institution has as its objective the sanctification of ordinary life while remaining in the world, in one's own sphere of work and in one's profession: to live the Gospel in the world, living immersed in the world, but to transform it and redeem it through the love of Christ himself. Yours is truly a high ideal, for from the beginning it anticipated the theology of the laity, which was to be a characteristic of the Church of the Council and after the Council'.

3

The Legal Question

FINDING THE RIGHT SUIT

Something new

On 2 October 1928, Father Escrivá had seen quite clearly that 'holiness is not something for the privileged few. Our Lord calls everyone; he expects Love from everyone. And that means all, wherever they may be, whatever their calling, their job, or their position .... People do not have to leave their normal role in life to seek God ... since all paths of this earth can be an occasion for meeting up with Christ', he wrote in 1930. Ordinary men and women are to seek God and to be apostolic in and through their commonplace work. Opus Dei represents a general mobilisation of Christians attempting truly to ratify the consequences of their baptism. Each then carries them out in the ordinary circumstances of civil life, reminding relatives, friends, colleagues, and chance and other acquaintances that 'they can be saints in the midst of all the noble concerns of this life. Sanctity is something accessible to all'.

These men and women, whether exercising brain or brawn, whether married or single, were and continue to be normal ordinary Christians who, with a stable dedication, by divine vocation and not on an impulse of the moment, try, thus, to grow in personal friendship with Christ. They strive to be contemplatives in the middle of the world and to make Christ known to others. In March 1934, the founder wrote that its aim was not to solve the sad situation of the Church in Spain', nor to 'fulfil the particular needs of any one country or period of time. From the start, Jesus has wanted his Work to have a universal, catholic heart'.

Opus Dei was not to be a temporary structure or organisation, but something permanent, with a characteristic unity of vocation, of spiritual-apostolic training and of government. It was to be made up of a group or portion of the Lord's flock, eminently secular (having its own secular priests and ordinary lay people) and worldwide rather than defined by territorial boundaries.

Opus Dei's message was so new that it simply did not fit in any of the Church's traditional moulds. Whenever there was talk of 'vocation', churchmen were used to thinking of the religious way of life. If it was to be a body for lay people, they immediately thought of associations of the faithful. The founder set about the task of elaborating the ascetical, juridical and theological doctrine wherein the Work might fit. The 1917 Code of Canon Law was unable to accommodate his foundational charism. Indeed, in this the canons reflected the general teaching of the time that conceived the Church as structurally divided along lines defined by different states in life. But Father Escrivá was certain Church law would ultimately devise a proper place for Opus Dei.

Full of faith in January 1932, he wrote to the first members: 'Remain faithful, and help me to be faithful and patient. We do not need to rush anything because, since our Lord has willed his Work, in his own time he will bring about the juridical solution, which cannot be seen at the moment. And Holy Mother Church will recognise our divine way of serving her, which will be in the world ... without any privileges and maintaining the essence of our vocation. Nor will we be counted among the religious, since it is our Lord who does not wish this for us'. This quotation adds one more feature to the form the juridical solution would take: Opus Dei would find a place in the *general* law of the Church, a place that would accommodate other institutions as well, and so the Work would not occupy a position based on exception or privilege.

As Father Escrivá saw it, law followed life. In the history of the Church, he pointed out, it was not a matter of rigid, prefabricated rules to which life had to conform. The Church was a living, divine body endowed with charisms by the Holy Spirit. Law was at the service of charism – not the other way around. Therefore his policy was to press on with his work, supporting it with prayer and penance, putting his trust in God. Everything would fit into place in due course.

In those first years, he saw that this general mobilisation of Christians, which had its own ways of doing things, needed a structure or organisation designed for ordinary Christians: something secular, personal and based on a charism or special vocation from God, which would specify and develop the vocation inherent in baptism and common to all Christians. A small episode reveals the direction in which his mind was working in his search for the juridical solution. One day in 1934, Pedro Casciaro, a member of the Work subsequently ordained, was waiting for the founder in St Elizabeth's Church in Madrid. He began to translate to himself the inscriptions on two tombstones at his feet. Just then Father Josemaría came out of the sacristy and pointing to the slabs said: 'That is where the Work's eventual juridical answer can be found'. The slabs carried the epitaphs of two prelates who had held a unique and wide-ranging ecclesiastical jurisdiction of a secular type, which was not territorial but personal. The founder would still have to sow his seed far and wide before such a formula could become a reality. This formula would not be a kind of privilege (literally a 'private law') designed for the jurisdiction enjoyed by the two prelates mentioned. Rather, it would be a personal, non-territorial structure, in the general law of the Church, open to people of all kinds.

HIERARCHICAL APPROVALS

Diocesan steps

A man who fully respected the Church's authority, Father Escrivá always wished to show in word and deed his submission to the hierarchy. With the Holy Spirit's assistance, the hierarchy alone is competent to assess the authenticity of various charisms. 'Do not stifle the utterances of the Spirit ... and yet you must scrutinise it all carefully, retaining only what is good' (1 Thess 5:19-21). For these reasons, when Father Escrivá began his work, he counted always on the permission and encouragement of his and Madrid's bishop, Leopoldo Eijo y Garay, and also of the Vicar General, Don Francisco Moran. The complete novelty of this new pastoral phenomenon gave rise to a whole series of misunderstandings that grew with the development of Opus Dei's apostolate. When these misunderstandings became more organised and systematic, Madrid's bishop felt the Work needed some kind of formal ecclesiastical approval and suggested Father Escrivá have it established as a Pious Union, a form of association of the faithful recognised by the Code of Canon Law. Bishop Eijo y Garay granted this approval on 19 March 1941.

Even in 1928, the founder had foreseen that there would be priests in Opus Dei, and he realised it needed priests of its own as soon as possible. These would come from the ranks of lay members. They would have not only a good ecclesiastical education, but also plenty of professional experience in secular work. They would also be well formed in Opus Dei's spirit. Such priests would be able to provide the specific spiritual attention and the doctrinal-religious instruction needed by the growing number of members of the Work. Church law decreed that nobody could be ordained unless his lifelong financial upkeep with minimum dignity could be guaranteed. Also to be solved was the question of juridical stability. This legal assurance is known as the 'title of ordination'.

None of the titles envisaged for secular priests was applicable to Opus Dei. Apparently it was God who provided a solution on 14 February 1943. Within Opus Dei, priests would have a title of ordination under the Priestly Society of the Holy Cross, of which they would be members.

At the request of Madrid's bishop, the Holy See in 1943 gave a mild form of approval (*appositio manuum* is the technical term). A *nihil obstat* was granted on 11 October 1943, to enable the bishop of Madrid to give official status to the small group of Opus Dei members who were training for the priesthood. This move set them up as a society of common life without vows. On 8 December 1943, canonical status was granted to the Priestly Society of the Holy Cross. The founder was very careful to point out in various documents that the term 'common life' was not to be understood in the canonical sense but rather in a new and wider sense. In other words, it was understood as a unity or a community of spirit and not in the physical sense of living under the same roof.

With this and other clarifications, he was able to safeguard the secular character of the priests. He was also very careful to ensure that the juridical form, rather than smothering the initial inspiration, would enable Opus Dei 'to move forward, safeguarding the essential, which cannot be changed', as he wrote on 14 February 1944. This step was simply a move in the right direction. Other Opus Dei members, men and women, remained ordinary Christians, secular lay people who formed their own association of the faithful, tied to the Priestly Society of the Holy Cross.

In the same document, the founder once again reaffirmed in writing that Opus Dei is not 'a new version of the religious state, adapted to present circumstances'. He was not trying to create 'a new canonical status', which would be 'something completely contrary to the essence of our vocation .... It is precisely the opposite: in other words, you have to retain the same state in life you had when the divine call to Opus Dei reached you'.

The same 1944 letter explained why the Priestly Society of the Holy Cross had come into being. After referring to the reasons given above – the need for priests, and specifically priests who would come from within Opus Dei – he added a further reason. This is something he had explained in earlier documents (e.g., Letter of 1 April 1934). He said these priests would, 'have some responsibilities of government ... a fundamental point in the very constitution of the Work ... strictly necessary for the juridical form appropriate for us'. These words give us a glimpse of the fact that the founder was thinking of an ecclesiastical structure in which priests and lay people would form a single body, but in which the principal positions of authority, since this was an ecclesiastical structure, would need to be held by priests: men who could administer the sacraments.

The solution of having a society of common life without vows, to which an association of lay faithful was linked, was 'the only viable solution within the limits available in the established law, and so we are ready to give way in the matter of words, provided that ... we affirm in a precise way the true nature of our path'. This solution is 'necessarily transitory, although it may have to do for some time, and it will be superseded as soon as a different juridical path becomes available'. Father Escrivá did not hide the difficulties implied by this new canonical arrangement and remarked: 'This solution is uncomfortable because the main thing – Opus Dei – appears in second place'.

With this step, he could count on a handful of priests to look after a group of the faithful, ordinary Christians. Later, some of them could occupy positions of authority. Up to this point, Opus Dei's setting had been diocesan. To spread it would need a broader approval, from the Holy See.

To Rome

In 1946, the founder sent to Rome for a second time Alvaro del Portillo, one of the first priests, to negotiate for pontifical approval. He was to try to obtain a juridical statute of universal right that, among other things, would make it clear that the priests incardinated in the Priestly Society of the Holy Cross and the lay members of Opus Dei formed a single organic and indivisible pastoral entity. On acquainting himself with the newness of Opus Dei', a high-ranking Prelate of the Roman Curia commented: 'You have come a century too soon'. In spite of being seriously ill, the founder travelled to Rome in June of the same year to pursue the matter.

Since 1940, studies had been going on in the Roman Curia to develop a new legal structure to accommodate various new apostolic initiatives, particularly certain associations of 'consecrated lay people' founded by Father Gemelli, O.F.M., of Milan. Since no other suitable solution existed, Opus Dei's founder agreed to a suggestion to come under a proposed Apostolic Constitution that was already in advanced draft form, to enable the Work to get the necessary statute to work on a worldwide basis. He was assured that the new kind of grouping would be a 'more secular' form than the societies of common life without vows, which were equivalent to the religious institutes.

Meanwhile, the Holy See granted a series of spiritual benefits to Opus Dei members with the apostolic brief *Cum Societatis* of 28 June 1946. On 13 August of the same year, a document came out that was an 'approval of the aims' of Opus Dei. It highlighted the 'sanctity of, the need for, and the opportuneness of the aims and apostolate' of the Work. On 2 February 1947, Pope Pius XII established Secular Institutes through the Apostolic Constitution, *Provida Mater Ecclesia*.

The 'Decretum laudis' of 1947. Part of this Constitution was open to a theological interpretation at variance with the foundational charism of Opus Dei. For example, even though the secularity of these Institutes was clearly expressed, the Constitution described them as religious in substance *(quoad substantiam)*. Thus, it required as a condition for any institute's approval, the so-called 'consecrated life', involving profession of the three evangelical counsels of poverty, chastity, and obedience taken as sacred bonds, vows, or pledges. Years earlier, the founder had written: 'We are interested in all the virtues ... but we are not interested in promises or vows, even though these are theologically worthy of every respect, and indeed we regard them in others with great respect' (8 December 1941).

To become international, Opus Dei needed pontifical approval. This would give it a universal and centralised juridical framework capable of guaranteeing unity in its government and spirit, in accordance with its apostolic growth. Since it was impossible to find a better formula among existing laws, the Holy See, at the founder's request, established Opus Dei as a Secular Institute with the Decree, *Primum Institutum,* of 24 February 1947. This approval gave God's Work the universal juridical framework noted above. It also confirmed its faculty to incardinate priests.

On 29 December 1947, Father Escrivá wrote regarding this new development: 'Once again in the effort to see our juridical position crystallise, to get closer to the model we need, I have been forced to accept certain things, accommodating ourselves to the letter of the law and to what is possible; but always waiting for everything to work out better next time, until we reach the ideal juridical position that will enable us to serve the Church and souls without any fear of our spirit being frustrated by unsuitable laws'.

In the same letter, he added: 'Up to now, we have gone where we never wished to go, though convinced that these wanderings are the route God wants us to take ... in the firm conviction and hope that everything will work out, because it is for the good of the Church and society. We must, however, pray to our Lord to provide the right solution, and we must take all the steps necessary to get off this sidetrack and start walking along a wide and sure road. When that moment comes, some people may tell us that the track – the one we are treading now – cannot be changed. It most certainly can! Every step, every human position can be changed, even if it has been around for centuries'. Throughout the letter, he often adverts to the danger that the provisions of *Provida Mater Ecclesia* might in practice gradually become more equivalent to a 'religious state', and that 'then our position would become much more uncomfortable and perhaps intolerable'.

Besides, the form of a Secular Institute could accommodate other aspects of Opus Dei only by making them an exception to the general rule and by granting certain privileges. This was distasteful to the founder. Two such aspects in particular were: first, unity, not only of spirit and training but also of jurisdiction and government for men and women, priests and lay people of the Work, ordinary Christians. Second, identity and fullness of vocation of all members, irrespective of family situation and other personal circumstances, and irrespective of availability to help in organised apostolic projects over and above each one being an apostle in his own milieu.

The Decree, 'Primum Inter', of 1950. Despite these limitations, the juridical progress of the Work had to go ahead, extending the legal framework so as to contain everything the Lord was asking for. Some form of Vatican approval moreover might silence, or at least attenuate, the organised campaign of misrepresentation of Opus Dei that had by now reached Rome. On 8 December 1949, Monsignor Escrivá wrote: 'In conscience we cannot but move ahead, making sure we overcome this compromise, that is to say, we have to give in without giving up; we must leave things in God's hands; he writes straight with crooked lines; he will enable us to reach our goal'.

For this reason, in February 1950, he asked the Holy See for another approval. On 16 June 1950, with the recommend-

The Venerable Josemaría Escrivá blesses a child in Buenos Aires in 1974. People of all kinds belong to Opus Dei: priests and lay people, men and women, young and old, married and single, of all occupations and professions. Most members are married with families.

The cause of beatification and canonisation of the founder of Opus Dei was opened in 1981. He was declared Venerable in 1990 and in 1991 the Holy See formally recognised as miraculous a cure attributed to his intercession, thereby opening the way for his beatification.

Torreciudad, a new shrine to the Mother of God, was an initiative of the founder of Opus Dei. Built alongside the site of an eleventh century Marian Hermitage, it lies 200 kilometres from Lourdes, south of the Spanish Pyrenees. Monsignor Escrivá's love for the Blessed Virgin played a central and decisive role throughout his life (see pages 110–111).

Midtown, an educational undertaking of the Opus Dei Prelature, provides young men of Chicago's heavily ethnic Near West Side with a rare combination of sports activities and personal attention in mathematics, reading and good study habits.

Started in 1965, Valle Grande (see pages 95–96), a corporate initiative of Opus Dei, is a farming school and training centre whose area of activity covers the Canete and Yauyos provinces of Peru.

At the request of Cardinal Gilroy, Archbishop of Sydney, members of Opus Dei in 1970 established Warrane College, a hall of residence for 200 students on the campus of the University of New South Wales, Australia (see pages 98–99). The site was provided by the University, and the building was financed by grants from the Federal and State Governments and private donations.

Bishop Alvaro del Portillo, Prelate of Opus Dei, with Pope John Paul II. Opus Dei was established as the first personal Prelature of the Catholic Church in 1982.

ation of 110 bishops from 17 countries, including 12 cardinals, the Decree, *Primum Inter*, gave its approval to the legal norms governing Opus Dei, and at the same time, as the founder sought, to the fundamental traits of the Work. The spirit these embodied was the key to the correct interpretation of the legal norms, still not adequate to the charismatic reality of the Work.

This approval, however, gave Opus Dei greater stability, scope for apostolic activity, and means to defend itself. Its fully secular spirit was approved in a much clearer way, as also the position of the Priestly Society of the Holy Cross. Thus, the unity between priests and lay members was highlighted. Although not yet in a fully satisfactory way, juridical entry into Opus Dei was also extended to people who for long had belonged to Opus Dei in spirit, if not in fact: people of every walk of life, married, widowed, or celibate. Non-Catholics and even non-Christians were also to be welcomed as co-operators. Priests incardinated in various dioceses were able to join the Priestly Society to receive spiritual coaching, without any detriment to their canonical and ministerial links with their respective bishops.

A most important step had been made; but unresolved problems still remained. There was always the risk of other difficulties arising from the kind of general interpretation given to the norms governing secular institutes. These interpretations often took, as a point of departure, the religious state or, in a wider sense, the 'state of perfection', or the 'state of consecrated life'. To protect Opus Dei from this danger, a rescript was issued by the Sacred Congregation for Religious on 2 August 1950, granting Opus Dei's founder and his Council permission to propose to the Holy See modifications and additions to the approved legal norms, when this appeared necessary and suitable to the development, needs, and extension of its 'excellent and unique apostolate'.

Inappropriateness of Secular Institute formula. Clearly, approval as a Secular Institute was unsatisfactory, all the more so owing to the widespread and growing tendency to view members of institutes as a modern kind of religious and to apply to them criteria proper to religious orders. Always loyal to the Church, Monsignor Escrivá wrote on 24 December 1951, ' ... For as long as there is no danger of deforming our spirit ... we have to defend the juridical form of Secular Institute until it is no longer feasible in conscience to do so'.

This letter is a particularly significant document in which the founder makes ample reference to juridical questions. Thus, speaking of the final solution, he says: 'I do not know, I repeat, when the time will come for the proper juridical solution, for which I pray so much and for which I urge you to pray .... I do not know when this moment will be and I imagine it will take many years, yet I am absolutely sure that it will come .... I will not accept a solution that involves exceptions or privileges, but rather a canonical formula that will enable us to work in such a way that the reverend bishops, whom we love "in deed and in truth", will continue to be grateful for our work. The bishops' rights will remain as now, quite firm and secure, and at last we will be able to follow our path of love, commitment, and dedication without useless obstacles being placed in the way of our service to the Church, that is to say, service to the Pope, to the dioceses, and to all souls ....

'When this final and truly decisive juridical solution is promulgated, our situation has to be absolutely clear: we are not religious nor can we be considered in any way equivalent to them. We are Christians who live consistently with our faith and who are ready to put it into practice at every opportunity. The lay people will do this by means of a normal civil contract [with Opus Dei] and they will practise Christian virtues in line with the spirit and statutes of the Work. They will undertake to do this for a certain period of time or for life. The priests additionally will have to live the consequences deriving from their priestly ordination and their incardination into the Work'. This text foreshadows, as do many others from Monsignor Escrivá, a canonical formula that did not exist at the time but that would come into being with the personal Prelature.

In several later documents addressed to his followers, Opus Dei's founder echoes these ideas. A letter of 19 March 1954 reads: 'We are not, in fact, a Secular Institute; neither do we form an "association of the faithful" whose members have no mutual or permanent bond with their respective societies. Nor can we be confused with "apostolic movements"'. Then, writing on the thirtieth anniversary of Opus Dei's founding (2 October 1958), he first explains why 'in fact we are not a Secular Institute and will not in the future describe ourselves as such'. Then he speaks of his decision to ask for a new juridical status from the Holy See. 'I shall inform the Holy See at the appropriate moment about this situation, this concern. At the same time, I will make known that we ardently desire that a suitable solution be found, which will not involve granting us a privilege – something repugnant to our spirit and outlook – nor will it change our present relationship with local bishops'.

While he shared these reflections, he informed the Roman Curia, both verbally and in writing, of the strains created by the present situation. For example, only weeks after asking for the 1950 approval, he had to express his respectful and firm protest against a recent decree in which the Sacred Congregation of the Council renewed its prohibition on priests and religious engaging in business, and specified that this law also applied to 'members of the recent Secular Institutes'. At times he sought provisional solutions through the granting of favours and dispensations. Although these averted one difficulty or another, they meant that Opus Dei was being treated 'differently', gradually acquiring an extraordinary or unique legal status, contrary to the founder's express wishes.

FINAL SOLUTION

Early 1960s

As we have seen, by the early 1960s, Opus Dei had an organisational structure of universal reach, with a centralised government presided over by the founder, to whom the Holy See had granted an authority that, for all practical purposes, was jurisdictional. The institution likewise had its own specific apostolic task, clearly secular and lay, namely, to help people understand and respond to the universal call to holiness, specifically sanctity in and through ordinary work carried out with a contemplative and apostolic spirit. To carry out this mission, Opus Dei counted on a portion or grouping of the faithful – clerics and lay people, men and women, married and single – who formed together an organic pastoral unity, all sharing the one vocation. However, this unique charismatic and social reality, unprecedented in the Church's history, was not adequately institutionalised.

The founder set about seeking a definitive solution, trusting in God and in the Blessed Virgin's intercession and also counting on Opus Dei members' prayers and mortifications long earmarked for this intention. He was also urged on by his conscience. He felt he had a duty as founder to see God's will carried out. Signs of the times also seemed ripe: Vatican Council II was about to begin ....

On 5 March 1960, Pope John XXIII received Monsignor Escrivá and Father Alvaro del Portillo in audience. On 14 March they met with Cardinal Domenico Tardini, Secretary of State. On 9 April Father del Portillo presented the cardinal with a petition from the founder to set in motion the juridical solution capable of resolving the institutional problem affecting Opus Dei. Already in this request mention was made of a Prelature and of its coming under the Sacred Consistorial Congregation (now the Congregation for Bishops). There was no official reply. Despite this silence, the founder was heartened because, as he said, 'a seed has been sown and it cannot fail to bear fruit'. On 7 January 1962, a new formal petition was presented to Pope John XXIII on the advice of Cardinal Pietro Ciriaci. The founder took all these steps despite strong interior resistance. As a good lawyer, he knew that the existing law would need to be stretched considerably to accommodate prelatures of a personal nature. This time the Pope replied by saying the request could not be granted in view of existing legislation. The reply was provisional in nature. Already preparations for Vatican II spoke of a new legal structure, later to be known as personal Prelature.

Pope John XXIII died in June 1963. When Paul VI was elected, the Work's founder, both directly and through Father del Portillo, renewed his negotiations with the Holy See. On 24 January 1964, the new pontiff received Monsignor Escrivá for the first time in a private and very cordial audience. (They had known each other since 1946.) A few days later (February 14), the founder sent the Pope a letter in which, among other topics, he pointed out the need for a solution to Opus Dei's institutional problems without making an official request. The pontiff had an answer sent to him that implied that the basis of a solution to the problem lay in the Council documents. In each of these approaches to the Holy See, a very clear statement of the founder emerges that no type of privileged arrangement was being sought. Moreover, he wanted relations with the diocesan bishops to remain substantially the same as before without any detriment to their rights. In a letter of 25 May 1962, he wrote to members detailing these and other traits of a possible solution.

Vatican II

Vatican Council II and the legal documents applying the conciliar decrees effectively opened up a suitable juridical configuration in the general legal setup of the Church.

The Decree, *Presbyterorum Ordinis,* dated 7 December 1965, declares that it may be useful to create personal Prelatures 'for particular pastoral activities for various social groups at regional, national, or worldwide levels'. This Section 10 of the decree was made operative by Pope Paul VI with his *Motu Proprio, Ecclesiae Sanctae,* of 6 August 1966. This document declares that, in order to carry out particular pastoral or missionary tasks, the Holy See may find it useful to establish Prelatures of this kind, made up of priests of the secular clergy, governed by their own Prelate and having their own statutes. As well as laying down rules regarding the Prelate's duties toward his own clergy and the Prelature's relations with other church authorities, Paul VI adds that 'there is no reason why lay people, single or married, who have made an agreement with the Prelature, should not dedicate themselves to the service of the works and initiatives of the Prelature, using their professional talents'.

Finally on 15 August 1967, the Apostolic Constitution, *Regimini Ecclesiae Universae,* which reorganised the Roman Curia, foresaw that personal Prelatures would be subject to the Sacred Congregation for Bishops.

Following Years

In 1969, Monsignor Escrivá called a special general congress of Opus Dei, after informing Pope Paul VI of his intention and receiving his encouragement. Studies were then initiated to effect the change of Opus Dei into a personal Prelature in accordance with its nature and the ordinances of Vatican Council II. The founder drafted new statutes in readiness for the time when it would be suitable to present them to the Holy See.

Though Monsignor Escrivá died in 1975 and Paul VI three years later, these studies were not interrupted. They received confirmation and encouragement from John Paul I and John Paul II. On 3 March 1979, Pope John Paul II asked the Sacred Congregation for Bishops, whose responsibility it was to study the matter, to examine Opus Dei's request and to take into account 'all the data of law and of fact'.

In an article published on 28 November 1982, in *L'Osservatore Romano* Cardinal Baggio, the Congregation's prefect, explained what this involved. 'Data of law': since the *Motu Proprio* contains norms for a general law or fundamental statute for personal Prelatures, what was being requested was not a privilege to be granted (which Opus Dei had not asked for), but an attentive evaluation of those general norms to see whether it would be correct to apply them in the specific case under consideration. 'Data of fact': the establishment of a Prelature was to stem, not from abstract doctrinal speculation, but rather and above all from a careful consideration of an already existing apostolic and pastoral entity whose legitimacy and foundational charism had often been recognised by Church authorities.

This study took three and a half years and went through four stages: 1) A working session of the Congregation's working assembly examined the matter in general on 28 June 1979. 2) A technical committee was set up, meeting 25 times between 27 February 1979 and 19 February 1981; the group examined all aspects of the matter including historical, juridical, pastoral, doctrinal, apostolic, institutional and procedural.

3) The Holy Father studied the committee's conclusions (600 pages in two volumes) and the proposed statutes of the future Prelature. John Paul II decided to submit these conclusions to the collegial deliberation of a special committee of cardinals. This committee reported back to the Pontiff on 26 September 1981.

4) Before proceeding to the Prelature's establishment, the Pope decided that a document outlining the essential characteristics of the Prelature should be sent to all bishops in whose dioceses Opus Dei had already established canonically erected centres. The communication went out to more than 2,000 bishops and invited their unhurried comments. The responses were few in number; each was studied care-

fully and given detailed replies. Meanwhile, the statutes drafted by Monsignor Escrivá were further examined. 'The study confirmed their validity and soundness and clearly showed the foundational charism of the Servant of God and his great love for the Church', wrote Monsignor Costalunga, an official of the Congregation.

This lengthy study having removed 'all doubts about the grounds for, the possibility of, and the specific form of an affirmative reply to the request, the suitability and useful-ness of Opus Dei's transformation into a personal Prelature became quite apparent,' declared John Paul II.

Becoming a Prelature

On 5 August 1982, Pope John Paul II approved a Declaration of the Sacred Congregation for Bishops that explained the fundamental traits of the Prelature as contained in its bylaws sanctioned by the Holy See. On 23 August the Pope decided to erect Opus Dei as a personal Prelature. On 28 November *L'Osservatore Romano* published the Declaration, signed by the Prefect of the Sacred Congregation for Bishops and its secretary, Msgr Moreira Neves. The Vatican paper also published an article by Cardinal Baggio entitled 'A Benefit for the Whole Church' and a commentary by Monsignor Costalunga, undersecretary of the Congregation ('The Erection of Opus Dei as a Personal Prelature').

On 25 January 1983, the Pope promulgated a new Code of Canon Law that contains a special section (canons 294-297) on personal Prelatures.

On 19 March of that year, the Prelature of the Holy Cross and Opus Dei was officially inaugurated at the Roman basilica of St Eugene. The Pope's Nuncio to Italy, Arch-bishop Romolo Carboni, represented the Pope at this act. The ceremony consisted of the promulgation and handing over of the Apostolic Constitution, *Ut Sit*, of 28 November 1982, by which Opus Dei was erected as a Prelature. The Constitution also approved Opus Dei's statutes (a particular code of law). On 2 May 1983, the *Acta Apostolicae Sedis* published *Ut Sit* and the Declaration (vol. 75, pp. 423–425 and 464–468).

A complete history of this whole legal question is available in the book *El itinerario juridico del Opus Dei* ('The juridical itinerary of Opus Dei') by Fuenmayor, Gómez-Iglesias and Illanes, Eunsa, Pamplona 1989. An Italian translation was published by Giuffre, Milan in 1991, and an English translation is in preparation. The book includes the full text of Opus Dei's statutes.

STATUS OF PERSONAL PRELATURES

What they are

Personal Prelatures are structures whereby limited and secular jurisdiction is exercised over a group of Catholics by virtue of each person's voluntary incorporation to the body; that is, the criterion of inclusion is not based on a defined territory (the usual case with dioceses). They are created by the Holy See to carry out specific pastoral activities within a region, country or throughout the world.

To fulfil its specific pastoral mission, each Prelature is to have its own Prelate (canonically its 'ordinary', whether a bishop or not) and secular priests, trained in the Prelature's seminaries. It is foreseen that lay people, through agreements made with the Prelature, may devote themselves to its different activities and initiatives in a manner established by the particular regulations in each case.

The Council documents and the more explicit subsequent pontifical documents indicate, among other things, that the establishment of personal Prelatures should come about after consulting the episcopal conferences of the territories concerned. This is done in line with the procedures laid down for each of these institutions and following their own particular statutes given by the Holy See.

These statutes are required, moreover, to fulfil a further stipulation of the Council. The bylaws governing each prelature must always respect the rights of the diocesan bishops and ensure that each Prelature's activity is harmoniously integrated with the pastoral work of the universal Church and of the local churches (see *Annuario Pontificio*).

Within the juridical framework of the Church, personal prelatures perform a pastoral function that can be carried out in a particular diocese only with the prior agreement of the respective bishop.

These characteristics distinguish personal prelatures both from particular churches (dioceses) and from associative institutions (institutes of consecrated life, societies of apostolic life, associations of the faithful). This is so even though a personal Prelature has some of the same constitutive elements as a diocese (Prelate, incardinated secular clergy, and in this case lay people who take full part in the apostolic activities of the Prelature and who form its *coetus christifidelium*); and even though there is no reason why an associative phenomenon would not later give rise to a personal Prelature.

Personal prelatures, thus, newly belong to the Church's constitutional structure and are governed by the common law of the Church. This is reflected in the way they appear in the new Code of Canon Law. As such, they are not based on privilege or exemption. Thus, they part company with the territorial prelatures set up under the 1917 Code and also with personal dioceses, which are fully independent from local churches and their respective diocesan bishops. The most common example of a personal diocese is that set up to minister to members of the armed forces and their relatives wherever they are found.

Opus Dei Prelature

Nature: It is a personal Prelature with its own statutes, of international scope, with headquarters in Rome and dependent on the Sacred Congregation for Bishops. The chapel of Our Lady of Peace, where the founder is buried, forms part of Opus Dei's headquarters (at 75 Viale Bruno Buozzi in Rome) and has been designated the Prelature's church.

The proper ordinary of the Prelature is its *Prelate*, currently Monsignor del Portillo. He has ordinary power of jurisdiction over the clergy incardinated in the Prelature and over the laity incorporated into it. In the latter case, jurisdiction extends only to the fulfilment of the specific obligations these lay people have undertaken as a result of their contract with the Prelature. Both clergy and laity depend on the Prelate's authority in carrying out the specific apostolic tasks of the Prelature.

The Prelature's clergy or *presbyterium* is made up exclusively of priests who have come from among Opus Dei's lay members. Thus, no priest or candidate for the priesthood is taken from any diocese. Opus Dei's priests depend exclusively on their Prelate, but they must observe norms issued by the diocesan bishops for the general discipline of the clergy and also all the territorial dispositions applicable to the generality of Catholic faithful.

The Prelature's *laity* can be men or women, single or married, from all levels of society, from any occupation and family situation. They receive a specific vocation to dedicate themselves to the particular apostolic tasks of Opus Dei. They depend on the local bishop, as defined by Church law (in this they differ not at all from other members of the faithful), according to the Prelature's statutes. Their dependence on the Prelate is limited to things having to do with Opus Dei's purposes.

The Prelature's *relations* with the Church's territorial *hierarchy* are laid down by its statutes, as the Code of Canon Law prescribes for such cases (canon 257). The diocesan bishop must be informed before the Prelature can begin regular activities in his circumscription. His acquiescence is an indispensable condition for Opus Dei to erect in his territory one of its centres. He has the right to visit centres erected canonically, to inspect the chapel, tabernacle, and place for confessions. The Prelature's priests require permission from him to carry out their ministry with faithful who do not belong to the Prelature. In each country, the Prelature must maintain frequent and regular contact with the president of the episcopal conference and with the bishops in whose dioceses it works. And should a bishop wish to entrust a parish to the Prelature, he will enter into an agreement with the Prelature.

Its purpose: A pontifical document makes clear that the Opus Dei Prelature has a double purpose. 'The Prelate and his clergy carry out a particular pastoral work in the service of the Prelature's laity, who are clearly defined; while the whole Prelature, clergy, and laity together engage in a specific apostolate in the service of the universal Church and of the local Churches.

'There are, therefore, two fundamental aspects of the structure and purpose of the Prelature, which constitute its *raison d'etre* and explain how it fits naturally into the whole of the pastoral and evangelising activity of the Church:

'On the one hand, the particular pastoral work that the Prelate with his clergy undertakes, in assisting and sustaining the lay faithful incorporated into Opus Dei, in the fulfilment of the specific ascetical, formative and apostolic commitments they have taken on, which are particularly demanding; and

'On the other hand, the apostolate that the Prelature's clergy and laity, inseparably united, carry out in helping to bring about, in all sectors of society, a deep consciousness of the universal call to holiness and apostolate and, more specifically, an awareness of the sanctifying value of ordinary work'.

Priests already incardinated in other dioceses do not form part of the Prelature's clergy. They may, however, join the Priestly Society of the Holy Cross, an association of clergy linked to the Prelature and erected by the Holy See at the same time as the Prelature. These diocesan priests in effect respond thereby to a new vocation to seek holiness by carrying out their pastoral ministry according to Opus Dei's spirit. Their diocesan status remains unchanged, as does their dependence on their respective bishops. They have no internal superior in the Priestly Society of the Holy Cross, so no problems of double obedience can arise. As is true of every association, they are subject to the internal regulations of the association, which in this case refer only to their spiritual lives. Opus Dei's Prelate also serves as the Society's president-general.

OPUS DEI'S ORGANISATION

Central

The Prelate is chosen by an elective congress summoned for this purpose. The election requires papal confirmation. The Prelate must be a priest with at least five years of ministerial experience. He may appoint an auxiliary vicar.

The Opus Dei Prelature is an undivided organic pastoral entity. As the Prelature's ordinary, the Prelate governs with the help of two councils, one for men and the other for women. The Prelate is aided in his charge of directing the apostolate with men by a General Council made up of an auxiliary vicar, if appointed, a vicar general, a vicar for the apostolate with women (called the central priest secretary), three deputy secretaries, one delegate at least from each of the Prelature's territorial units, a prefect of studies, and a general administrator. The auxiliary vicar, vicar general, and central priest secretary are all chosen from the priest members. A procurator, who must be a priest, represents the prelature before the Holy See, and a central spiritual director watches over the common spiritual direction of all the prelature's faithful, under the direction of the Prelate and his councils.

The council responsible for apostolate with women is governed by the Prelate with his auxiliary vicar, vicar general, central priest secretary and the Central Advisory, similar in form and function to the men's General Council. All the directors of these two organs of government are appointed for eight-year terms (with the exception of the auxiliary vicar).

Regional and local

The Prelate, with the agreement of his councils, sets up regions or quasi-regions, which are governed by a regional vicar, appointed by the Prelate with the concurrence of his council. In turn, the vicar is assisted by two councils, one for men and the other for women. These councils are organised in a similar way to the central councils. Again, every canonically erected centre of the Prelature is governed by a director with a small committee. Between the regional vicar (with his councils) and the respective centres, sometimes there may be intermediate bodies called delegations. They help to govern a segment of a region and its respective centres. These delegations are headed by a vicar delegate (a priest) assisted by his councils.

4

Opus Dei Members

WHO THEY ARE

Diverse yet one

To join Opus Dei presupposes a true, supernatural vocation. It is a personal, intimate call from God to put one's whole life at his service, in keeping with Opus Dei's spirituality and by making use of the circumstances each one finds in the world.

A *single vocation:* Often did Monsignor Escrivá stress how all Opus Dei members receive the very same calling to be holy and apostolic in the exercise of their work. Consequently, there are not different levels of dedication in the sense that some members are more important than others or have received a more demanding vocation. Regardless of circumstances, he emphasised complete equality. Not only are there priests and laity, men and women, married and single, but the lay members come from all levels of society, and from all races, and work in the most varied professions. Thus, when Opus Dei reaches its maturity in a country, it presents a socio-professional composition highly-representative of the country in question.

Singleness of vocation means that all the faithful of the Prelature – the priests included – take on the same ascetic and apostolic commitments and receive the same doctrinal formation. It is important to see the way in which the common priesthood of all the faithful and the ministerial priesthood of the clergy complement one another to achieve the unique apostolic objective of Opus Dei.

Diversity of members: Within this single vocation (which the founder likened to a single 'cooking pot' into which everyone can dip according to his needs), there is a variety of types of members, which basically express diverse personal situations and modes of availability of those who ask to be members of the Prelature.

The *Numeraries* are those members (men and women) who have received a call from God to live apostolic celibacy and collaborate with all their efforts and their complete availability in carrying out the specific apostolic tasks of Opus Dei. They normally live in centres of the Prelature, so that they can look after the formation of the other faithful of the Prelature and direct apostolic activities. Some male *Numeraries* and *Associates* are called to the priesthood and, once ordained, comprise the clergy of the Prelature.

The *Associates* are lay faithful of the Prelature who place their whole lives at the service of God in apostolic celibacy, according to the spirit of Opus Dei.

However, owing to circumstances of a personal, familial, or professional nature, they usually live with their families.

Supernumeraries are lay faithful, single or married, who give themselves fully to God in their particular state in life – having the same divine vocation as the numeraries and associates. They play a full part in Opus Dei's apostolic activities insofar as these are compatible with their family, professional, and social duties. Like all the other faithful of the Prelature, they seek to make of their occupations and social relationships a means of holiness and apostolic efficacy. But, like the associates, they do so in their homes and in keeping with their family duties.

Co-operators are those who, without being Opus Dei members, collaborate apostolically through prayer, donations, gifts, and even work. They partake of the Work's spiritual benefits and constitute an association that works alongside the Prelature. Non-Catholics and even non-Christians can be co-operators.

Priests

The Prelature's clergy: Opus Dei priests are drawn from lay members who, after completing third level studies (in the case of all numeraries and some associates) and prescribed ecclesiastical studies (to doctorate level in one of the sacred sciences), have been called to the priesthood by the Prelate. They come from the Prelature's lay ranks where they have received all their training and education. Opus Dei does not, therefore, take away from the territorial Church any priests or candidates to the priesthood.

These members then give up the profession they have practised perhaps for many years, to become 'priest-priests, not priests more or less, but priests one hundred percent', following the founder's express will. The vocation to Opus Dei is the same for all; and so, for an Opus Dei member the priesthood is not like the crowning of an apostolic career. Rather, it is viewed as a call to continue serving souls, though in a different way from the laity.

Opus Dei priests receive their training in centres the Prelature establishes for this purpose, following norms laid down by the Holy See. Either personally or through his vicars, the Prelate gives priests their canonical mission and their priestly faculties, first and foremost, to look after the activities and the faithful of the Prelature. This includes the sacrament of penance or reconciliation, respecting, of course, each person's right to go to any confessor he wishes. Besides this pastoral care of lay members, the Prelature's clerics, like all its faithful, try to carry out extensive and deep apostolic work in the service of the universal and local Church. They foster a recognition of the universal call to sanctity in fulfilling one's everyday work.

The Prelate must provide for the adequate support of his clergy and for their care in case of sickness, incapacity, or old age. He also encourages them to keep close links with the clergy of the territory where they exercise their ministry and to live a deep fraternity with them. Opus Dei priests feel themselves to be – as in fact they are – diocesan priests in whichever diocese they work. They belong by full right to the diocesan *presbyterium.*

According to the Pontifical Yearbook, the Prelature's clergy now number over 1,300 priests. Ordinations take place regularly and involve in recent years some 50–60 priests annually. Ordination to the priesthood has been conferred notably by Cardinals Koenig, Hoeffner, Oddi, and Law and by the present pontiff (June and November, 1982, and June 1983–91).

The Priestly Society of the Holy Cross: This is an association of priests, of the type called for by the Second Vatican Council in its Decree, *Presbyterorum Ordinis.* The Society aims to foster holiness in fulfilling the priestly ministry, providing its members with ascetical and spiritual coaching and, thus, helping them to maintain, among other things, an exemplary availability and responsiveness to the requests of their bishops and to the dioceses' needs.

Priests incardinated into Opus Dei are automatically members of this Society. In addition, deacons and priests already incardinated in a diocese may join the Society, in response to a vocation to live their ministry in their diocese according to Opus Dei's spirit, while remaining entirely and exclusively dependent upon their bishop. They try to make their own the motto, *nihil sine Episcopo* (nothing without the bishop), and to practise fraternity especially with the other priests of the local clergy and with all priests. Among these they seek to foster priestly holiness and to encourage complete submission to the ecclesiastical hierarchy who, thus, find their authority reinforced.

Lay people

Number: At the end of 1990, the lay faithful of the Prelature (divided more or less equally between men and women) numbered over 75,000 of 87 nationalities. Most of them are married and live with their own families. A vocation is a personal calling, so it is often only the husband, or the wife, or one of the children, who belongs to Opus Dei.

Variety: The lay members come from all social levels and occupations. The fact that there is a large number of manual and clerical workers in Opus Dei obviously does not attract the attention of some of the media, which tend to be much more interested in socially prominent members. For the founder, however, 'the vocation of a railway porter is as important as that of a corporation executive'. And the ideal of holiness proclaimed by Opus Dei in practice finds a strong response in rural as in urban settings, in westernised societies, and in those steeped in eastern, African, or other traditions, in strongly Christian areas and in pagan or mission countries.

Within the same vocation to apostolic holiness, Opus Dei unites doctors, lawyers, miners, bricklayers, artists, politicians, farmers, housewives, film directors, teachers, academics, manual workers, fishermen, small shopkeepers, industrialists, craftsmen, air pilots, research workers, nurses, members of the armed forces, cleaning ladies, taxi drivers, hairdressers, models, journalists, cattle dealers, judges, technicians, union officials, railwaymen, athletes, philosophers, policemen, diplomats, writers .... There is no danger of elitism because 'out of every hundred souls', Monsignor Escrivá used to say, 'we are interested in all hundred of them'.

It is worth pointing out that, in spite of such great diversity of members, there is no difference or distinction made among any of them. Here, undoubtedly, is a characteristic of Opus Dei that further explains why it was erected as a personal Prelature, and the appropriateness of its place in the ordinary hierarchical and pastoral structure of the People of God.

Relations with bishops: The laity, following the Prelature's statutes, depend on (or are subject to) the bishops of the place where they live, in accordance with the norms of Canon Law, exactly like other faithful, their equals. Their dependence on the Prelate applies only to areas that refer to the specific aims of Opus Dei. The training and coaching they receive from the Prelature serves to strengthen their union with the bishop and other pastors of their local Church, because it helps them in their efforts to be exemplary Catholics.

They try to venerate their bishops; they show them affection and seek to encourage the same sentiments among other faithful. They contribute, as far as their personal circumstances permit, to carrying out the pastoral directives of the diocesan bishops and of the episcopal conference. The same is true of their relations with parish priests.

INCORPORATION INTO OPUS DEI

Joining Opus Dei

There is a minimum age of 18 years. There is no maximum age; people over 80 have received a vocation. Incorporation into the Prelature of the Holy Cross and Opus Dei is brought about by a mutual and stable bond of a contractual nature between the Prelate and the lay faithful who choose to join it. (The situation of the Prelature's clergy is the same as that of the laity, for they join Opus Dei as laymen and only receive Orders later on). To underline the secular character of this incorporation, the Declaration of the Congregation for Bishops specified that it does not have the force of a vow. The commitment of Opus Dei members is, thus, radically different in its nature from that of religious and of consecrated persons who profess the three vows of poverty, chastity, and obedience. The state in life of Opus Dei members is therefore completely unaltered by their belong-ing to the Prelature; the total absence of a sacred bond means that each person remains an ordinary lay member of the faithful in the diocese to which he belongs.

Their link with Opus Dei is effected by means of a formal, contractual declaration made bilaterally in the presence of two witnesses. By this declaration, the Prelature promises to provide continual training and guidance in doctrinal, spiritual, ascetical, and apostolic matters, as well as personal pastoral help from the Prelature's priests; and to fulfil the other obligations to the faithful of the Prelature determined by the norms governing the Prelature.

The member in question – the other party to the contract – freely declares that he is firmly resolved to seek holiness with all his strength and to be apostolic according to Opus Dei's spirit. He promises to remain under the Prelate's jurisdiction and of those who help him govern the Prelature and thereby to devote himself to the aims proper to it. He further pledges to fulfil all the duties of his condition as an Opus Dei member and to follow all the norms of the Prelature and the indications of its authorities in matters of its government, spirit, and apostolate. This he promises until the contract is renewed or for the rest of his life, as the case may be.

Leaving

No one remains in the Prelature against his will. Everyone is there, as the founder said, 'because he feels like it, which is the most supernatural of reasons'. He made it quite clear that while a person needs to knock insistently on the door to be admitted, the door is wide open to let him leave. This is not to say that people are not helped to persevere with the appropriate spiritual guidance.

Commitments

The Declaration cited above specifies that the members' personal commitments are 'ascetical, formative, and apostolic'. These refer to specific areas recognised by the Church where all Catholics enjoy autonomy in their actions and where each person can exercise his legitimate freedom and personal responsibility. These commitments bear on matters that were not previously subject to any ecclesiastical jurisdiction, precisely because they are areas where the faithful are free.

The commitments entail obedience to the Prelature's directors, an obedience undertaken freely and which Monsignor Escrivá described as 'voluntary and responsible'. It is marked by a spirit of initiative characteristic of human beings who are 'neither stones nor corpses', but 'intelligent and free'.

The *ascetical* commitments involve following a programme of spiritual life. While demanding, this programme is adaptable to the personal circumstances of each member. It leads him progressively 'up a gentle slope' to find God in his everyday work and in his other activities.

The plan comprises an intense sacramental life, centred on daily Mass and Holy Communion, plus weekly confession; daily reading of the New Testament and some spiritual book; rosary; examinations of conscience; monthly day of recollection and yearly retreat; constant seeking of God's presence; frequent consideration of one's divine filiation; spiritual communions; spiritual aspirations; and so forth.

In addition, every member should maintain a spirit of mortification and penance, including corporal mortification in keeping with the age, health, and circumstances of each. This is in line with a practice in the Catholic Church that goes back to Christ himself, involving methods approved by the Church and carefully avoiding all excesses.

Special importance is accorded to daily work as a true hub of holiness and apostolate. It is within their work that Opus Dei members try to develop human or natural virtues – diligence, spirit of service, honesty, loyalty, self-sacrifice – as well as supernatural virtues. These commitments are reinforced by both personal and collective spiritual guidance.

The *formative* commitments cover, among other things, a religious education that never ends for Prelature members, again in accordance with individual possibilities and capacities. This facet aims at nourishing each person's spiritual and apostolic life, combining 'the piety of children with the sure doctrine of theologians'. Thus, the hope is that there be people in all areas of society intellectually equipped to spread good doctrine effectively in the exercise of their profession or trade.

This training, more concentrated during the first years of incorporation into the Prelature, is given individually or in courses for homogeneous groups. The Prelature's directors are careful to see that the time given to doctrinal classes does not cause neglect of family or professional duties.

Philosophical and theological instruction is given to all members as far as their personal, family, and occupational circumstances permit and warrant. In accordance with the Prelature's statutes, this training carefully follows the Church's teaching authority. In conformity with the norms established by Vatican II and by the Holy See, this education is based on the teachings of St Thomas Aquinas. Opus Dei has no doctrine of its own and does not form its own schools of thought on the philosophical, theological or canonical issues the Church leaves open to free discussion.

The *apostolic commitments* lead the Prelature's faithful to carry out the common duty of all Christians to be apostolic in a practical, constant, and effective manner. These apostolic efforts have two aspects: first, bringing the knowledge of Christ and his teachings to those who do not yet know it; and, second, encouraging Christians to respond to the God-given invitation to holiness in executing the duties of their state in life and of their everyday work.

In keeping with Opus Dei's spirituality, the call to be apostolic is not seen as an activity to be added on to various others or to be carried out only at certain times. The apostolic dimension is an essential part of the Christian vocation *per se*. It follows then that it must be continuous and intense, an integral part of a Christian's response to all the situations arising in everyday life.

In their dealings with friends, colleagues, and so on,

Opus Dei members seek to communicate religious truths and dispel ignorance. A number of them feel motivated to live apostolic celibacy so as to be entirely available for this teaching, while also giving witness thereby to other essential truths. The Prelature's statutes stress that its members' apostolic activities should always make use of supernatural means first and foremost. Moreover, each must respect the legitimate freedom of others' consciences.

MEMBER'S LIFE

Normal Christians

To those who wanted to understand the lives of Opus Dei members and to have a clear point of reference to start from, Monsignor Escrivá used to say that 'the simplest thing to do is to think of the lives of the early Christians', who incarnated Christianity in their lives and naturally spread it around them.

A member's life is the same he led before he joined the Prelature. It keeps the same family framework; it takes place in the same occupational and social setting. Monsignor Escrivá explained that 'an essential characteristic of Opus Dei's spirit is that it does not take anyone out of his place. Thus is echoed the Pauline teaching: "let everyone remain in the state in which he was called" (1 Cor 7:20). On the contrary, it leads everyone to carry out his task and duties of state as perfectly as possible'. The Prelature's faithful are not people who live apart from the world and enter it to work as labourers, businessmen, or whatever. They are labourers, businessmen, or whatever, with their own professional interest and outlook, who view work and relating to others as ways that lead to God.

To put it another way, no one, on answering a call to Opus Dei, changes his normal way of life, his ordinary work, or his plans. That is a characteristic of Opus Dei, which has 'the strangeness of not being strange', as the founder put it.

Only a small number of celibate members live in the Prelature's centres so as to be available for other members and managing apostolic activities, while continuing to work at their jobs. They live a family life in the centre that resembles in so many ways the home and life of a normal Christian family.

External conduct

An Opus Dei member cannot be distinguished from his colleagues in any way. 'We are identical to others, not "like others"', wrote the founder in 1930, 'and we have, in common with them, their concerns as citizens, and those proper to our trade or profession, and other typical interests; the same kinds of background, the same ways of dressing and behaving'.

Since they are ordinary Christians and not religious, members dress like anyone else in their position, with nothing odd or eccentric about them, adapting their schedule to the demands of their activities, usually living with their families, and so on. Opus Dei does not set out to create or spread special ways of doing things – not even special kinds of prayers. It tries to bring its members and all those who benefit from its spirituality to put into practice the spiritual and apostolic demands of the Christian faith. The personality of each member is not just respected but strengthened and enriched.

Opus Dei's spirituality lays stress on the role of the person, both in his own sanctification and that of others. It is open to creative ideas; there are no typical activities proper to Opus Dei, no collective demonstrations, no stereotyped approaches or group behaviour.

Naturalness

Naturalness steers members away from making a show of their membership. 'It would be repugnant for them to carry a placard on their backs saying: "Let it be known that I am committed to God's service". That would be neither lay nor secular'. On the other hand, neither do they hide or disguise the fact that they belong to the Prelature. Those who know them recognise that they are members, for their daily life and apostolic efforts plainly witness to it.

In the open

If personal apostolate of individual members is carried out in the open, this is even more so with the corporate apostolic ventures of Opus Dei, organised in and from its centres officially and publicly known to be such. This way of being apostolic does not depend on any spectacular or propagandist means. It is characterised by the naturalness that comes from realising that 'Jesus Christ has made holiness the condition for effectiveness in apostolic activity', and that their lives would make no sense if they were not redolent of prayer and an eagerness to bring souls closer to God. To work in this way, grand strategies are not needed, nor will closed, regimented approaches avail. Every member tries to work effectively, without drawing attention to himself, with the same naturalness with which Jesus hallowed his everyday life in Nazareth, while no less effecting the redemption of the human race. The members also try to be collectively humble, which is why Opus Dei works with so little fuss.

Opus Dei functions everywhere with the legal recognition and consent both of the civil and ecclesiastical authorities, the latter as foreseen in the Declaration. The names of directors and priests, and the educational and apostolic activities of the centres are public knowledge, easily found in all the relevant directories and yearbooks.

CORPORATE UNDERTAKINGS

What they are

Opus Dei's basic message is an invitation to holiness in the middle of everyday activities. Its members' apostolate is therefore primarily a personal 'apostolate of friendship and trust'. Nevertheless, for apostolic reasons, some Opus Dei members sometimes join forces with their friends, including people outside the Church or any church, to set up 'corporate' works of apostolate. These activities are always professional and lay in character; they radiate the warmth of Christian spirit and also contribute to resolving problems in specific areas of education, welfare, and personal and social development. If those who manage these centres so request, Opus Dei as such sometimes assumes their chaplaincy, in which case they can properly be called 'corporate' apostolates of Opus Dei.

These corporate apostolates are always initiated and directed by ordinary citizens exercising their normal rights. They are responsible for everything but the chaplain's ambit: planning, development, finances, personnel, quality control, relations with outside authorities. They are lay citizens doing ordinary, secular work, just like their colleagues in a similar job or trade.

As their directors are at pains to point out, these activities, even with their apostolic inspiration, are not Church activities, officially or unofficially. They are simply private initiatives run with a lay, secular outlook. They are set up and develop following the needs and customs of each place, without privilege of any sort. They come under the same regulations as activities promoted by any other citizen, foundation or association. The people who run them are directly responsible to the appropriate civil authorities.

These corporate activities try to accommodate themselves to the needs and circumstances of a given location. Ultimately, it is society that benefits most.

Features

These corporate works mirror the essential traits of Opus Dei. They are directed above all towards a spiritual purpose: always plainly apostolic, they operate in the fields of teaching, social services, human development, and so on. They could never be industrial or commercial activities such as businesses, publishers, newspapers, or banks. Activities of the latter type could certainly constitute the personal professional work of members, but in this case they are personally responsible and Opus Dei has no say or influence in them. The Prelature cannot take any responsibility, even indirectly, for anyone's job, be it designing a bridge, making a film, or selling a product.

The directors of corporate apostolates try to help those who take part in them to develop their personalities to the full, without pressuring anyone. 'An apostolate that did not completely respect freedom of consciences would certainly not be right', wrote Monsignor Escrivá. All those who attend activities know they can benefit, if they so wish, from the doctrinal and religious training and guidance made available to them. They learn to use their personal freedom in an upright manner (and, if they are Christians, with a supernatural sense), to respect others' freedom and to shoulder their own responsibilities. Thanks to this environment of freedom and responsibility, participants feel spurred to work well and eagerly.

These activities are open to men and women, boys and girls, of all backgrounds, with no discrimination by reason of social status, race, religion, or creed. This openness extends not only to those attending activities, but also to those who manage them and work there. Non-Catholics who frequent such centres find an atmosphere of understanding, respect, and friendship. In order to develop, a person needs to live with others and share experiences. And there is no fellowship worth the name without respect for everyone's freedom. A natural sense of human solidarity prompts one to put personal talents at the service of others lest they turn rancid in self-service. In these centres a genuine family life develops, and those who feel at home often feel motivated also to explore Christianity, owing witness to the faith lived by those they find there.

Finances

The success of Opus Dei's apostolate is based on God's grace and, on the human side, on much prayer, work, and self-sacrifice. But financial resources are also needed. By their very nature, apostolic activities are never profitable. And less so when they are aimed at people with little or no resources. These centres are able to keep their doors open, thanks to four sources of funds.

First, each corporate work relies on its own resources: tuition in the case of a school or academic centre; fees for room and board in the event of residence halls; income from the sale of produce or the sale of arts and crafts in vocational or agricultural centres.

Second, members give part of what they earn from their job to support these undertakings. Each gives what he can: there is no fixed quota representative of different kinds of members, nor do individual members commit themselves to paying a fixed amount. Each periodically looks at his own situation and, following his conscience, sees what he can give towards the upkeep of the apostolic activities.

Third, and above all, there are many generous people, including Opus Dei co-operators, who contribute what they can. Some are spiritually motivated; others, apart from the apostolic aspects, are attracted by the social dimension of these initiatives and their contribution to the common good.

Finally, these activities are the recipients of grants from private foundations and public agencies, inasmuch as they carry out educational or social work that relieves society and the government from part of their obligations.

Some examples

Vocational Training: ELIS Centre (the initials stand for education, work, instruction and sport) in the industrial Tiburtino district of Rome is run for young men training to become technicians or craftsmen. Pope John XXIII decided to entrust to Opus Dei members the realisation of a social work financed with donations made on the occasion of Pius XII's eightieth birthday. Coming in person to inaugurate the centre in 1965, Pope Paul VI declared, *Tutto, tutto qui è Opus Dei* (Everything here is Opus Dei, the Work of God). Pope John Paul II expressed similar sentiments when he visited ELIS in 1984.

The centre houses 140 students (apprentices, craftsmen, technicians, employees, and young people undergoing work training). Four-fifths of them receive partial or full scholarships. One in ten comes from beyond Italy: Africa, Middle East, the Third World generally. The residence is organised in units of 16 or so, to keep things on a human scale and to foster a family atmosphere.

The Technical College trains 250 workers in electro-mechanical engineering, technical drawing, data processing, numerical control, and so on. Its own workshops occupy 300,000 square feet of space. Since it was launched, nearly 2,500 young men have graduated from its programmes. The courses are free, underwritten by various public bodies. The centre also organises courses for foreigners as part of programmes of technical aid set up by the Foreign Ministry (two-month courses in English, Spanish, or French for foremen and training co-ordinators, and eight-month courses for instructors in mechanical and electro-mechanical engineering).

The facilities provided by the ELIS Sports Group and School cover 200,000 square feet and give over 300 youngsters annually a basic grounding in different sports, particularly soccer and basketball. They also take part in tournaments and even international competitions.

A youth hostel, accommodating 60, welcomes groups from throughout the world. Apprentices and students make use of the hostel when visiting Rome for congresses, tourism, and the like.

An experimental state secondary school was opened in 1980 and now has three grades and nearly 100 pupils (this number seems set to rise, given circumstances in the Tiburtino district). ELIS Club, for boys 10–14, fosters personal friendship, develops character and inculcates a habit of serious study among its members. An Information Centre and Library promotes reading and cultural development and houses a reference collection for the vocational centre. There are also activities for parents, such as courses on family development.

Independently of these activities, women members of Opus Dei look after the adjacent *Scuola Alberghiera Femminile Internazionale,* which offers training and placement in the fields of catering and institutional housekeeping. The complex also houses the church of the local parish of St John the Baptist, entrusted to Opus Dei priests.

Other initiatives of this type elsewhere include: *Centro de Capacitacion Obrera Kinal* in Guatemala City; *Instituto de Desarrollo Personal* in Mexico City; *Midtown Center* in Chicago; *Monteverde* in Bogota; *Tajamar* in Madrid; *Centro Cultural y Deportivo Oeste* in Buenos Aires; and *Centro Tecnico* (CETEC) in Sao Paulo.

Farm Schools: For people in rural areas there is, for example, the *Instituto Rural Valle Grande* in San Vicente de Canete in Peru, a centre giving technical training in agriculture and animal husbandry. It works throughout the central mountain ranges of Peru and the corresponding coastlands – an area of some 6,000 square miles and up to 18,000 feet above sea level.

Since 1973, *Valle Grande* has greatly expanded its work by setting up *Escuelas Radiofonicas Americanas* (radio schools). It has 365 listening posts scattered among the villages; it broadcasts courses in aspects of farming, animal husbandry, general culture, Christian values, and so forth.

The *Instituto Rural* has an auditorium seating 200, classrooms for 600 students, and a residence for 30. It fosters all-round growth by means of technical training, co-operation and development, social teachings of the Church, etc. Life in the residence during the intensive courses aims to help people avoid rivalries and to nourish new friendships – so necessary in the sierra where life is very tough indeed.

Courses cover methods of improving farm yields, bee-keeping, family poultry farming, cattle vaccination, pruning and grafting of fruit trees, cheese-making, and use of insecticides and fertilisers. It has soil testing laboratories, provides agricultural advisory and veterinary services, and helps in community projects such as irrigation systems. Every year, some three thousand people involved in farming receive direct training, thus benefiting the general population.

Valle Grande gets half of its financing from the sale of its poultry farm and beekeeping programme and from the services furnished by its two laboratories. The rest comes from Peruvian and foreign agencies for aid and rural development. Almost all the activities of the *Instituto Rural* are, thus, more or less free: only a token fee is asked for so that those attending can better appreciate and value the help they receive. With help from the Italian government, *Valle Grande* has developed the *Club Cultural y Deportivo Azor* for boys of the area between nine and seventeen years, and the Paracan Medical Post for first aid, preventive medicine, and research into regional diseases.

Other centres along the same lines include: *Las Garzas* in Chile; *Instituto Tecnico Agrario Bell-lloc* in Gerona, Spain; *Escuela Agropecuaria el Penon* in Morelos, Mexico; and numerous family farming schools.

Educational Centres: When it opened its doors in 1961, *Kianda Secretarial School* in Nairobi, Kenya, was the first multi-racial educational centre for women in Africa. It accepts 300 pupils annually, studying either for a one-year secretarial diploma (typing, shorthand, commercial English, business management, etc.) or for a two-year bilingual (English-French) secretarial degree. Of the thousands who have passed through Kianda, almost a third have come from beyond Kenya's borders. One fifth of the young women receive scholarships. Graduates generally have no trouble finding immediate work. Hence, they can quickly begin to help their families. Often, they are a family's only bread-winner, since many come from large, rural families. Through contact with the school, a number of Kenyan families have discovered and embraced Christianity.

As a social service, Kianda's students give classes in reading and writing to local people and visit the sick and elderly. The teaching staff, composed mainly of past pupils, is trained at Milikiwa, a centre tended by Kianda. The School has also provided the expertise to help set up *Lagoon College* in Nigeria, run along similar lines.

Again in Nairobi the *Kibondeni School* was launched in 1967 to teach hotel management and home economics. Over 1,000 pupils have completed the two-year course for a Certificate of Institutional Management. The School also runs a *Home Economics Club* for girls in Nairobi and *Watani Hostel*, a residence hall for alumnae and domestic employees. Plans are afoot for another centre specialising in hotel management.

Kianda Residence also dates from 1967. It accommodates one hundred boarders, both from Kianda and other academic institutions. Nearly half the students come from outside Kenya. Again scholarship help is available.

Kianda High School began in 1977. The secondary school enrols some 360 students, a quarter of whom are foreigners from 15 other African countries. The school sponsors annual-ly a French essay competition and likewise takes part in the Kenya Music Festival, scientific competitions, and the like. Great attention is paid to parental involvement and to up-grading the skills of the teachers themselves. Soon, a Kianda Primary School will open.

At Kianda, as at other centres, days of recollection, retreats, and courses in practical Christian living are held to give pupils the opportunity to deepen their faith and to make it accessible to others.

Now in its thirtieth year, *Seido Language Institute* is located in Ashiya, Japan. Every year 1,500 students (men and women from industry and higher education) participate in its highly acclaimed language courses, some of which last up to three years. English is by far the most popular, followed by French, German, and Spanish. Seido has developed an original method of teaching English that takes into account the particular difficulties experienced by the Japanese student. *Modern English: an oral approach* is now used by over 500 educational centres throughout the Japanese archipelago. The institute has also opened a publishing division to produce textbooks, tapes, a periodical digest of Catholic documents, catechisms, spiritual books, and so on.

Seido Institute also has a youth club. The Seido Overseas Summer Study Abroad Programme permits students to stay with families abroad while attending summer courses. Next to the institute is a *Cultural Centre* that, among other activities, makes the faith better known in a nation where Catholics are but a tiny minority. Of the 15,000 alumni of Seido a mere 300 have been Catholics.

A sampling of other youth clubs: *Turey Club* (Puerto Rico); *Tamezin Club* (London); *Ganunda Boys' Club* (Montreal); *Club de Valk* (Maastricht, Holland); *Frontier Club* (Roseville, Australia); *Club Montelar* (Madrid); *Club Xenon* (Lisbon); *Yalam Youth Club* (Hermosillo, Mexico); and *Centre of Studies for Women* (Brussels, Belgium).

Examples of schools and colleges are *Los Pinos College* (Quito, Ecuador); *Strathmore College* (Nairobi); *The Heights* (Washington); *Gaztelueta* (Bilbao); *Southridge* (Manila). Their numbers reach into the thousands.

Residence halls: One of the seven colleges on the campus of the University of New South Wales is *Warrane College.* Opened in 1970, it was the first Australian college to be run by Catholic university professors as a full-time job. Three-quarters of the construction costs were met by the government; the rest came from private sources. Over 2,000 students from 33 countries have passed through Warrane. A third of the residents receive scholarships, mainly from the state of New South Wales.

Warrane has its own traditions and style. An example is its 'orientation week' at the start of each new academic year for residents from different countries in Asia and Oceania. Students in their last year help run this introduction to life at Warrane and at the university. There are also athletic traditions such as the election of the 'Sportsman of the Week' – one out of Warrane's 200 students recognised for having defended Warrane's colours in intercollegiate competitions in any of 20 sports.

Most of Warrane's activities centre on complementing residents' university studies. There is a programme of tutorials in more than 30 subjects. Also, it offers a programme of professional orientation aimed at finding jobs. Many residents and non-residents (including non-Catholics) avail themselves of a wide range of spiritual activities. The collegians give catechism in local parishes and visit the elderly and sick.

The cultural life of Warrane College springs from residents' initiatives: talks, debates, musical get-togethers, outings, films, and so forth. Summer courses have been offered in computer studies, English language courses, and other offerings aimed at foreigners, from New Caledonia, for example.

A partial list of educational enrichment centres and residence halls found throughout the world are *Ashwell House*, London; *Studentenheim Wahring*, Vienna; *Pineda Cultural Centre*, Barcelona; *Ciudad Vieja University Centre*, Guatemala; *Layton Study Center*, Milwaukee; *Netherhall House*, London; *Alcor University Residence*, Madrid; *Imoran Study Centre*, Ibadan, Nigeria; *Steenberg University Residence*, Louvain, Belgium; *Studentenheim Schweidt*, Cologne; *Miravalles Study Centre*, San Jose, Costa Rica; *Grandpont*

House, Oxford; *Montefaro University Centre*, Montevideo; *Tanglaw University Center* Manila; *Residenza Universitaria Internazionale*, Rome; *Monteavila University Cultural Centre*, Caracas; *Alborada Residence and Cultural Centre*, Santiago, Chile; *Riverview*, Montreal; *Los Esteros Study Centre*, Guayaquil, Ecuador; *Nullamore University Residence*, Dublin; *Inaya Women's University Residence*, Bogota; *Studentenheim Fluntern*, Zurich.

Universities: The *University of Navarre* opened its doors in Pamplona, Spain, in 1952. Today it has grown to encompass faculties of law, medicine, philosophy and letters, pharmacology, natural sciences, canon law, theology, journalism, and economics. Also found there are schools of architecture, industrial engineering, library sciences, nursing, teaching, liberal arts, Spanish language, and literature. The university also runs eight halls of residence housing over 800 students.

Since its inception, over 31,000 students have graduated from Spain's first private university. In 1990 it had over 16,000 students, of whom 3,000 were carrying out postgraduate work. Less than two percent of the university's budget comes from public sources. A major source of funds is the nationwide association of Friends of the University.

Complementing the curriculum are a number of varied cultural and spiritual activities. The university's chaplaincy, for example, organises retreats, Easter conferences, various Marian devotions, plus facilitating Mass and the sacrament of penance.

The University Hospital comes under the faculty of medicine. It has over 500 beds. In the most recent year, over 10,000 patients were admitted, while over 60,000 outpatients were also tended to.

Since 1958, a unit of the University of Navarre has functioned in the Mediterranean port city of Barcelona. The *Instituto de Estudios Superiores de la Empresa (IESE)*, a graduate school of business administration, also offers intensive courses for active business executives. In collaboration with Harvard University, IESE has acquired an international reputation. At present, there are students from 34 nations studying there; over 750 graduated from it during the most recent academic year. Its alumni now total over 8,000.

The Roman Athenaeum of the Holy Cross, a centre for studies in the ecclesiastical sciences, was established by the Holy See through a decree of the Congregation for Catholic Education on 9 January 1990. It began in 1984 as the Roman campus of the University of Navarre, being established as an Athenaeum, or independent university, in 1990. It offers undergraduate and postgraduate programmes to men and women, clergy and laity, in philosophy, theology, and canon law.

Ediciones Universidad de Navarre (Navarre University Press) published nearly 100 titles in the most recent academic year. It also publishes nine specialised and scholarly reviews, ranging from medicine to theology.

Various activities are run by the university over the summer months: refresher courses for graduates, upgrading programmes for primary and secondary teachers, courses for medical students, intensive courses in Spanish language and literature, philosophy conferences, seminars on practical applications of canon law, and so on.

Other universities promoted by Opus Dei members are found in Peru, Colombia, and Mexico.

Home Economics and Conference Centres: In 1952, an old hacienda dating from colonial times became *Montefalco Conference Centre* (Morelos State, Mexico). Made up of three main buildings, it can now house 110 people at a time in separate groups: housewives, students, professionals, domestic employees, secretaries, manual workers, and so forth. Each year, 5,000 people avail themselves of the centre's programmes; more than 50,000 since it was started. The activities are organised largely by other corporate works of Opus Dei in Mexico.

In 1956, the *Centro de Estudios Montefalco* was added. This offers a two-year training course in catering and domestic work. Each of the 40 students receives a half scholarship, sponsored by a promoter group, and covers the rest of her expenses by the work she does. They also give training courses in many villages of the region.

Students at the above Centro also help as tutors in the *Escuela Feminina de Montefalco*, which opened its doors to rural housewives in 1958. In 1969, this rural school set up the *Telesecondaria* (a three-year secondary school broadcast on television), which enrols each year some 200 students. In 1978, a teacher training school began, offering a four-year programme to 135 students. Over 2,700 pupils have passed through the girls' school. Enrolment fees are very low: the school survives on monthly grants from a beneficent organisation. Besides professional training and religious instruction, the school gives special attention to character development, personal and domestic hygiene, care of food and clothes, deportment, temperance, a sense of responsibility, industry, and the like. The school takes part in activities at the community, state, and national levels: athletic competitions, conferences, exhibitions on literature, physics, chemistry, social science, etc. As a service to the local community of the Amilpas Valley, the Montefalco complex organises social, cultural, and spiritual activities in some 20 villages.

Its *Tonameyo Club* is attended by 140 young girls from the surrounding villages. They learn music, crafts, home economics, cooking, and dressmaking. They participate in conferences and outings. They also receive talks on spiritual and character formation. About 500 young people a year are prepared for first Communion.

Similar centres include: *Lakefield Catering and Educational Centre, London,* opened by the Queen Mother in 1966; *Crannton Catering Centre,* Dublin; *Ecole technique d'hotellerie Dosnon,* near Rheims (France); *L'Éssor, Centre de Formation pour la Femme,* Montreal; *Punlaan School,* Manila; *Mikawa Cooking School,* Nagasaki; *Escuela Tecnica de Formacion Profesional Besana,* Madrid; *Kenvale Training Centre,* Sydney;

Lexington Institute, Chicago; *Instituto de Capacitacion Integral en Estudios Domesticos,* Buenos Aires; *Hauswirthchaftlicht Ausbildungsstatte Mungersdof,* Cologne; *Wickenden Manor,* Sussex (England); *Lismullin Conference Centre,* Tara (Ireland); *Makiling Conference Centre,* Manila; *Shelbourne Conference Center,* Valparaiso (Indiana); *Thornycroft Hall,* Macclesfield (England); *Ballyglunin Park Conference Centre,* Tuam (Ireland); *Castello di Urio,* Lake Como (Italy); *Kimlea,* Tigoni (Kenya); *Iroto Conference Centre,* Nigeria.

Further information on apostolic activities of Opus Dei can readily be obtained from its information office in the corresponding country. In the United States its address is: 330 Riverside Drive, New York, NY 10025 (914-235-1201). The address in Ireland is 10 Hume Street, Dublin 2 (tel: 614949), and in Britain it is 5 Orme Court, London W2 4RL (tel: 221-9176).

The corporate apostolates of the Opus Dei Prelature must be carefully distinguished from many other cultural and formative activities that are also promoted and manned by Opus Dei members, but for which the Prelature assumes no responsibility. These are personal initiatives of members (either alone or with friends and colleagues) that normally constitute their professional work. Here the responsibility for the moral and doctrinal orientation, as well as the purely technical aspects, does not in any way rest with the Prelature but wholly and entirely with the promoters of the activity in full use of their responsible freedom as Catholic lay people.

5

Other Spiritual Facets

MONSIGNOR ESCRIVA'S WRITINGS

Opus Dei's founder was a prolific writer. 'My name is Escrivá,' he used to joke, 'and I write a lot' (playing on the Spanish words for scribe and to write: *escribir*).

He had undoubted literary talent. His writings in the original Spanish show precision and vigour. The style is unpretentious and avoids a facile appeal to the emotions. It employs a rich vocabulary and a use of imagery at times reminiscent of the Gospel parables.

A feature that runs through almost everything he wrote is the way he takes as a starting point something from Scripture, either the New or Old Testament. He meditated upon God's Word so as to 'get inside the scenes of the holy Gospels, to be just one more person among those present', Msgr Alvaro del Portillo has written. In this way Monsignor Escrivá brings out fresh insights and draws practical lessons, directly relevant to everyday life and accessible to every reader. His writings are also notable for their frequent quotations from the Fathers of the Church. Most of his published works include an index of references to Scripture, the Fathers and Doctors of the Church and to official documents of the Church, in addition to a subject index.

Published works

The Way has seen nearly 250 printings, in 39 languages, with a total run of 3,600,000 copies. Apart from the main European languages, *The Way* has also been published in Arabic, Armenian, Basque, Catalan, Croatian, Czech, Danish, Finnish, Irish, Greek, Hebrew, Hungarian, Japanese, Lithuanian, Maltese, Polish, Quechua, Rumanian, and Tagalog. There are also some Braille editions in various tongues.

The Way was first published in Cuenca (Spain) in February 1934 under the title *Consideraciones espirituales*. It acquired its present form with a few additions to the second edition, published in Valencia in 1939.

The book contains 999 points: the three-digit multiple of three being chosen in honour of the Blessed Trinity. A number of points come from letters written or received by the author; some are advice he gave to people; some come from things said by people who came to him for spiritual guidance; others spring from considerations he had formed in prayer or when reading the Scriptures or other books. *The Way* was born of the author's spiritual life and pastoral activity. With its often conversational style the work puts forward a vision of Christianity that constantly challenges mediocrity. Its appeal is directly to the reader's heart.

The first of its 46 chapters deals with character, with the human personality itself and the determination a Christian must have if he or she is to take life seriously, with the help of spiritual guidance which, in turn, becomes the theme of the second chapter. As the author encourages the reader along the path of prayer (chapter 3), he brings out the various facets of Christian and human life as they present themselves in the ordinary occurrences of every day: presence of God, interior life, sanctity as a goal, interior struggle, spiritual childhood, cultivating virtues, attention to little things .... The chapters of *The Way* trace out a journey of faith that culminates in the final pages. There the ordinary Christian's life is presented as the life of a child of God who knows he is called to take part in Christ's mission: 'life of childhood', 'calling', 'apostle', 'apostolate', 'perseverance'.

'Monsignor Escrivá has written more than just a masterpiece' *(L'Osservatore Romano)*. Interestingly enough *The Way* has been called *'The Imitation of Christ* of modern times'. The book's wide sales mean that it is playing a major role in establishing an appreciation of the supernatural value of temporal realities and in the formation and spirituality of lay people. The latest English printing is available from Four Courts Press (Dublin), Scepter (London and New York), and Sinag-tala Publishers (Manila).

Holy Rosary: First published in 1934, it has since seen many reprintings in 18 languages totalling 600,000 copies. This book is basically a meditation on each of the 15 joyful, sorrowful, and glorious mysteries of the rosary and concludes with some considerations on the Litany of the Virgin (Loreto). The author wrote it in one sitting, during his thanksgiving after Mass. The book is designed to help the reader share the joys and sorrows of his fellow men, to turn simply and confidently to Mary and through her to the Blessed Trinity. 'The beginning of the way, at the end of which you will find yourself completely carried away by love for Jesus, is a trusting love for Mary' (Prologue).

Conversations with Monsignor Escrivá: Starting in 1968, this collection of interviews has seen 311,000 copies produced in eight languages. This book gathers seven interviews Monsignor Escrivá gave to the press in the 1960s, such as *Le Figaro,* the *New York Times, Time, L'Osservatore Romano,* and other periodicals.

In it Monsignor Escrivá replies at length to questions by journalists, sometimes put quite bluntly, about Opus Dei's spirit, the Church (the Second Vatican Council had just ended), and respect for the rights and freedom of the individual. He also replies to questions about the idea of a university and women's role in society and the Church.

Conversations finishes with a homily entitled 'Passionately Loving the World', delivered in 1967 on the campus of the University of Navarre before a congregation of more than 30,000 people. The homily, notable for its profound spirituality, sums up Monsignor Escrivá's responses to the kind of questions raised in the earlier part of the book. He says, for instance: 'Authentic Christianity, which professes the resurrection of all flesh, has always quite logically opposed disincarnation, without fear of being judged materialistic. We can, therefore, rightly speak of a Christian materialism, which is boldly opposed to those forms of materialism that are blind to the spirit'. The most recent English printing was done by Sinag-tala Publishers (Manila).

Christ Is Passing By: First published in 1973, 64 subsequent printings in 11 languages have put 394,000 copies in print. This book contains homilies given between 1951 and 1971 on eighteen different feast days and arranged according to the cycle of the liturgical year.

It is a stimulating and profound exposition of doctrine and the Christian way of life. The underlying theme of divine filiation leads to the universal call to holiness, the sanctification of ordinary work, the dignity of secular life, contemplation in the middle of the world, unity of life, and so forth. The English translation, first published in 1974, is currently available from Four Courts Press (Dublin), Scepter (London and New York), and Sinag-tala Publishers (Manila).

Friends of God: This second collection of homilies saw the light of day in 1977. Available in eight languages, 293,000 copies have been published. Published posthumously, the 18 homilies, given between 1941 and 1968, aim at helping people to live in 'the friendship of God', a God who is close to the reader. This time it is a chain of virtues that forms the book's backbone.

Addressing himself to lay people seeking sanctity according to a specific vocation in ordinary life, Monsignor Escrivá proposes an interior life based on humility, presence of God, self-denial, converting work into prayer, purity, and a host of virtues that enrich the believer's soul and help him to grow in holiness, while likewise encouraging others to do the same.

In the foreword Monsignor del Portillo points out that it is not 'a theoretical treatise, nor potted hints for acquiring spiritual good manners. The homilies contain living doctrine and combine a theologian's depth with the evangelical clarity of a good shepherd of souls .... They provide, therefore, a lesson in doctrine and Christian life in which God is not only spoken of but spoken to'. The first English version became available in 1981.

The Way of the Cross: Since the first edition in 1981, there have been 306,000 copies printed in ten languages. Alongside the traditional presentation of the 14 stations that make up this devotion, five points for meditation taken from Monsignor Escrivá's preaching have been added to each commentary. Quotations from the Gospel and prophets enrich the text.

The book goes further than being an aid for the devout practice of the stations of the cross. Following closely our Lord's passion, the book offers abundant material for meditation and for contemplative life, by pursuing paths taken by Monsignor Escrivá himself throughout his life. [They] 'led him to the highest peaks of spiritual life', Monsignor del Portillo writes in the foreword. The first English translation dates from 1983.

Homilies: The homilies that appear in the two books already mentioned, as well as others – on the priesthood, the Church, and so on – have been published singly as booklets. Over two and a half million copies have been printed in 12 languages.

La Abadesa de las Huelgas: In a theological and legal monograph published in 1944 and reissued in 1974, Monsignor Escrivá studies an extraordinary case of quasi-episcopal jurisdiction exercised by the abbess of the famous convent of Las Huelgas (1187–1874) near Burgos in Spain. This book has not been translated into English.

Furrow and *The Forge:* Both of these works were published posthumously, the first English translation of *Furrow* appearing in 1987 and *The Forge* a year later. Similar to *The Way*, they are collections of points intended to spark and facilitate personal prayer. *Furrow* has seen 29 printings in eight languages, with a total of 288,000 copies, while *The Forge* has seen 19 printings in six languages, with a total of 257,00 copies.

Unpublished writings

There is still a great deal of unpublished material. There are letters and other documents addressed to Opus Dei members to help them in their apostolic work and spiritual life. There are also thousands of the founder's extant letters to people of all kinds, with whom he carried out a true 'letter-writing apostolate' throughout his lifetime. Monsignor Escrivá's works also include a large number of homilies and talks he gave to Opus Dei members and others.

Films

Special mention should also be made of other more recent and also unpublished material: films that were taken during the 'catechetical' get-togethers with thousands of people in the last years of the founder's life. They are particularly valuable, because they give people who never met Monsignor Escrivá the opportunity to see him 'live', very much as he was.

SPIRITUAL PROFILE

A study of the founder's various writings brings out other aspects of Opus Dei's spirit. While belonging to the Church's common patrimony, his teaching nevertheless has a particular flavour and throws a special light on the Christian's secular presence, both active and contemplative, in an increasingly secularised world.

Divine filiation

Monsignor Escrivá's entire teaching rests on one very profound conviction: men and women are God's children. He himself experienced this very vividly one day in the summer of 1931 on a tram in Madrid. He was pondering how to carry out the mission God had given him three years earlier. Amid no little anxiety but there and then he received a very clear reply that remained engraved as by fire on his soul. The voice borrowed words from the second Psalm: 'You are my son, this day have I begotten you'. His soul was so inundated with joy that he was unable to stop himself from repeating aloud: *Abba, Pater! Abba, Pater! Abba! Abba! Abba!* [While Pater obviously translates as Father, Abba in Greek comes closest to meaning 'Daddy'. Christ so addressed his Father several times in the Gospel.]

Later he was to write: 'Being God's son or daughter is a joyful truth, a consoling mystery. It permeates the whole of our spiritual lives. It allows us to get very close to our heavenly Father, to know him, and to love him. It fills our interior struggle with hope and confers on us the trusting simplicity of little children. But even more: precisely because we are God's children, this trust also enables us to contemplate, full of love and wonder, everything that comes from the hands of God, Father, and Creator. We are indeed contemplatives in the midst of the world, this world we love'.

Divine filiation is the bedrock foundation for all of Opus Dei's spirituality. When Monsignor Escrivá speaks of faith, he speaks of believing as God's children; when he refers to strength, he talks about the fortitude on loan to God's children. When he calls for conversion, he envisages God's children turning back to their Father ....

Devotion to our Lady

Monsignor Escrivá was very devoted to the Holy Family of Nazareth, whom he called the 'trinity on earth'. He saw the Holy Family as the path that leads to union with the Trinity. St Joseph takes us to Mary; Mary leads us to Jesus, who in turn enables us to rise up to the Father and the Holy Spirit.

The founder named St Joseph, patron of the Church and of workers, patron also of God's Work. He vigorously emphasised the key role the patriarch played in the Holy

Family. St Joseph is 'master of the interior life, since he teaches us to get to know Jesus and to live with him, and helps us realise that we belong to God's family. St Joseph teaches us all this by being what he was: an ordinary man, the head of a family, a working man who had to earn his bread by the sweat of his brow'.

Close to Joseph we find his spouse Mary. If there is one single trait that dominated Monsignor Escrivá's whole personality it was his love for the Blessed Virgin. His entire life and the whole of Opus Dei's story have been marked by favours from God's Mother – 'and our Mother too'. Convinced that 'Jesus can refuse nothing to Mary, nor to us who are children of the selfsame Mother', he invited people to 'put Mary into everything and over everything'. Thus, he taught, we always go to Jesus – and return to him – through Mary.

In Mary he identified also a woman who led a life similar to that of most women, like them busy with family chores and the task of bringing up children. 'Mary sanctifies all these things down to the smallest particulars, the things that many people wrongly consider unimportant and value-less: everyday work, dealings with people who love one another, conversations and visits with relatives and friends .... Blessed be an ordinary life that can be so filled with love for God!'

Unity of life

Being a Christian does not mean having a title we proudly sport. Rather, it entails being 'salt' and 'light' for all men (the call to be apostolic). This mission is not an accessory; it reaches us through baptism and helps us to act as God desires (the call to holiness). It means that we should act, not merely out of ambition, nor just for nobler aims such as philanthropy or compassion, but 'to reflect at its deepest and most radical level the love that Jesus Christ has shown to us' (freedom and responsibility).

It would not be right to reduce Christianity to a set of practices or acts of piety. 'We should see prayer's connection with ordinary life and feel urged to respond to others' needs, as we try to right various forms of injustice'.

Therefore, a Christian trying to be consistent with his faith cannot live a double life: living part-time a series of devotions, and then the rest of the time a godless life at work and play alike. He has to reach a 'unity of life, pure and simple' that makes him an 'all-round' Christian. He is then, for example, able to face social problems in a professional way, avoiding an improvised, amateur approach. Then through inner conversion he will influence social structures and, if he feels it necessary, work to reform them. It is in this spirit that Monsignor Escrivá promoted and encouraged a thorough education for even the neediest, since education equips them to shape their own social progress, and so ensure that their personal dignity is fully respected. 'It is in our own efforts to be better, to live an ever purer love, to rein in our selfishness, to give ourselves completely to others and make of our lives a constant service' that Christ manifests himself in us and we attain contemplation. Eventually it becomes impossible to distinguish 'where prayer leaves off and work begins, because our work is also prayer, contemplation'.

The Mass

Continual awareness of God's presence in the heart of ordinary activities comes about above all through participation in the holy sacrifice of the Mass. We are to see it not only as the unbloody renewal of Christ's sacrifice on Calvary, but also as the pact of each baptised person to imitate his redeemer. The Christian's 'priestly soul' derives from the common priesthood of the faithful, a participation in Christ's priesthood (though essentially different from the priest's ministry). It prompts Christians to make of their lives a continual praise of God. 'Thus, our lives are a prolongation of the previous Mass and a preparation for the next'. The layman's Mass 'lasts 24 hours'.

The Mass, thus, becomes 'the centre and root of the interior life', an expression taken up by the Second Vatican Council. One's life must be sacrificial to become identified with Christ. The Mass provides the divine energy that powers one's work, sanctity, and apostolate.

Opus Dei members endeavour to combine this 'priestly soul' with a lay outlook. 'It is with a fully lay perspective that you exercise this priestly spirit. Thus, you offer to God your work, rest, the joys and setbacks of the day, the holocaust of your bodies exhausted by the effort of uninterrupted service'. Souls consequently should strive to be turned, figuratively if not literally, toward a tabernacle, a 'prison of love'. There Jesus has been 'waiting for us for 20 centuries'.

Prayer

Prayer is the only weapon, the most powerful means, to conquer in the battles of the spiritual life. Without it nothing worthwhile or lasting can be achieved. Monsignor Escrivá wanted it to be 'the true prayer of God's children – and not the chatter of hypocrites.' It's to be a conversation full of love and simplicity in God's presence, in the depths of the soul. 'God's children have no need of an elaborate or set method to turn to their Father'. Here once again we have an echo of the 'Long live freedom!' that resounded so often in the founder's words and deeds. 'Love is inventive, ingenious. If we are in love we will know how to discover personal, intimate ways to dialogue continually with our Lord'.

At times prayer makes use of acts of love, ejaculatory prayers, passages from the Gospel. One needs to 'get to know' Christ in the Bread and in the Word, in the Eucharist and in prayer, Monsignor Escrivá used to emphasise. 'And we need to get to know him as we would get to know a friend, a real living person. That is what Christ is, for he has risen again'. Personally the founder did his utmost to be punctual to his fixed appointment to meet this Friend in prayer. It is an encounter dictated by love, and Christ should not be kept waiting.

Monsignor Escrivá saw mortification as the body's prayer. Mortification and penance are indispensable if one is to act in an upright way; they form the 'salt of our life'. Without them one cannot become a prayerful soul. He invited people to follow these priorities: 'First, prayer; then, atonement; in the third place, very much in third place, action'. Although he himself practised very exacting mortification, Monsignor Escrivá used to teach that the best mortifications are found in the little things of each day, while taking care not to mortify other people.

'You are not mortified,' he wrote, 'if you are touchy, if you listen only to the voice of your own self-centredness, if you impose your views on others, if you are not able to deprive yourself of what is superfluous and at times even of what is necessary, if you get downhearted when things do not turn out as you expected. On the other hand, you are mortified when you are able to make of yourself "all things to all men in order to gain all"'.

He used to give a whole series of other practical examples: to fulfil exactly the schedule one has set; not to leave more difficult tasks for later without good reason; to find time for all the things one has to do; to treat others with the greatest charity, beginning with those closest; to converse patiently with people who are boring or tiresome; cheerfully taking care of those who are sick or distressed; to interrupt and change plans when the good of others requires it; to endure with good humour the thousand small bothers of each day; to finish off properly any work we have undertaken, even if the initial enthusiasm has waned; to be detached from one's things; to reprimand and correct when necessary, as the matter requires and in line with the circumstances of the person who needs to be helped in this way ....

He also encouraged people to practise interior mortification, 'so our conversations do not revolve around ourselves, so that we always receive unpleasant things with a smile (which can often be the best proof of a spirit of mortification), so that we make life pleasant for those around us'.

Following their founder, Opus Dei members cultivate a spirit of mortification to purify themselves and to obtain genuine and lasting spiritual progress. It paves the way for an effective apostolate and shows by deeds their love for Christ, who delivered himself up to death on the cross out of love for men. Mortification, thus, becomes something joyful; the interior struggle is seen as 'smiling asceticism'. Self-denial leads to the cross, where Christ is found with his arms open wide, ready to welcome all men. 'If you seek Christ, could you want a surer sign than the cross to know you've found him?' When the cross is seen not so much as an instrument of torture but as a 'throne of triumph' upon which the redeemer won victory over death, sin, and the devil, the whole horizon flips: 'Isn't it true,' asks Monsignor Escrivá, 'that when you stop being afraid of the cross, of what people call the cross, and your will is set on accepting God's will, then you are happy? Then all worries and sufferings, both physical and moral, disappear'.

Hidden life

Opus Dei's spirit also aims at imitating the 30 years of Christ's hidden life, when he manifested his holy humanity. Those years are part of the redemptive process, if for no other reason than they occupy almost Jesus' entire life on earth. Because there is little mention of these years in the Gospels, it might appear at first sight that they are of slight importance. However, Monsignor Escrivá saw them as 'years of intense work and prayer. Jesus Christ lived an ordinary existence, similar to ours if you like, which was both divine and human'. Thus, nothing in a Christian's life can be

115

useless or unimportant. Life in Bethlehem or Nazareth was replete with the typical little tasks of home life. But if everything is done out of love, 'there will be no little things: everything will be big. Perseverance in little things for Love is heroism'.

Jesus is portrayed as subject to Mary and Joseph, two creatures as perfect as you wish, but creatures nonetheless and infinitely inferior to Christ. The obedience Monsignor Escrivá saw modelled there led him to write, 'To obey always is to be a martyr without dying'.

Humility is a precondition for obeying. God's greatness lies hidden in a stable, wrapped in swaddling clothes. God humbles himself so that men might draw close to him .... 'Our freedom gives way not only to the sight of his power, but also to the marvel of his humility'. Thus true self-knowledge becomes the touchstone of spiritual life. Insofar as one learns a little about himself, to that extent one realises one is little more than a rebellious instrument in God's hands.

Jesus' hidden life was also marked by poverty. Monsignor Escrivá outlined the characteristics of this virtue for people in the world who have to use material goods. He invited Prelature members to adopt the standard of 'a father of a poor and large family'. He emphasised that 'rather than in not having, true poverty consists in being detached, in voluntarily renouncing one's dominion over things'. He also pointed out that poverty should not be confused with scruffiness or bad taste, taking also in this regard a cue from Christ: 'Our Saviour wore a valued seamless cloak, he ate and drank like other people ... and everyone knew that he had earned his living for many years by manual work ... In short, I would say to you that we ought to wear clean clothes, to be clean in body – above all in soul'.

Virtues

A person who has encountered God should try to practise all

virtues. At baptism are received the theological virtues, which only God can increase. 'Lord, increase my faith, hope, and charity!' the founder would exclaim.

Charity is the first of the virtues: it constitutes the essence of holiness, since God is pure love. 'We have to drown evil in an abundance of good' by being concerned about the good of others and above all apostolically concerned about the good of their souls. Charity brings with it love of freedom, understanding, forgiveness, willingness to find excuses for others, love for others' defects (so long as they do not directly offend God), not judging others, considering oneself the enemy of absolutely no one. 'I didn't have to learn to forgive, because our Lord taught me to love', Monsignor Escrivá told his followers. Some of them, targets of strong opposition and attacks, wrote to him: 'Father, no need to worry: there is not even the slightest thought against charity amongst the lot of us'. He advised some students imprisoned during the Spanish Civil War to play soccer with anarchist prisoners. Not only would they show politics has no place in sports, but their Christian doctrine and example might just rub off on their political enemies.

Charity goes beyond justice. As soon as he learned during the civil war that a certain man who resembled him had been hanged in his stead in front of his mother's apartment, Father Escrivá began to pray for him in his Mass every day. 'We have to behave in such a way that when other people see us they can say: "He is a Christian for he is not a fanatic, for he dominates his passions, for he sacrifices himself, for he radiates peace, for he loves"'.

This genuine love calls for the practice of fraternal correction, pointed out by Christ in the Gospel and which 'savours of the dawn of Christianity'. By it one helps others overcome rough edges or defects and thus avoid situations that might otherwise undermine fellowship and friendship.

Faith disposes the mind to say 'Yes' to Christ, to renew the unconditional *Fiat* ('Be it done') that Mary spoke to the archangel Gabriel. 'It is all a matter of faith', the founder used to say in every situation, whether good or seemingly terrible. Why? 'Because *omnia in bonum*: everything works out for the good'. We must accept everything as coming from the hands of our Lord Jesus Christ. Monsignor Escrivá claimed God had given him a faith 'so thick you could cut it with a knife'. He had the faith to be able to speak about Opus Dei's future over the centuries and to speak with conviction at a time when everything still remained to be done. At the end of the first class in practical Christian living he gave to three students in January 1933, he saw 'three thousand of them, three hundred thousand, three million ... white, black, copper-coloured, yellow, of all languages and from every latitude ....'

Hope consists in the certitude that life has a meaning transcending the limits of this world. Thus everything – the tiniest sacrifice, the smallest act of love – can possess a value for all eternity 'in spite of everything', in spite of human meanness and equally human weakness. 'Cast away the despair produced by the realisation of your weakness. It's true: financially you are a zero, socially another zero, and another in virtues, and another in talents .... But to the left of these zeros is Christ. And what an immeasurable figure it turns out to be!'

Part of the virtue of hope is expectation of heaven. Towards the end of his life, when he was suffering from cataracts in both eyes, Monsignor Escrivá used to say, *Vultum tuum, Domine, requiram!*: 'I will seek your face, O Lord'. 'I like very much to close my eyes and think that there will come a moment, when God so wishes, when I will be able to see him, not as through a glass, darkly ... but face to face. Yes, my sons and daughters, my heart thirsts for God, the living God. When shall I see him face to face?' However, he did not as a consequence neglect his duties. Indeed for decades he had wanted to die very old, 'squeezed out like a lemon' (that is, having worked until he could give no more).

Faith, hope, and charity, along with the other virtues that accompany God's grace, move a Christian to nurture the qualities he shares with many others. These 'human virtues lie at the base of the supernatural virtues'. It would be impossible to list them all, but among them are some that have a special impact in the life of an ordinary Christian: loyalty, industry, simplicity, sincerity, naturalness, self-restraint, courage ....

We might pause to consider purity or chastity, a quality often caricatured and reduced to a series of taboos and prohibitions. Monsignor Escrivá saw chastity as 'a joyful affirmation'. It is a voluntary commitment of love that does not aim simply at avoiding falls or dangerous situations. Rather at the first stirrings of passion 'and even earlier', the chaste person steers away from danger and runs to God. Suggesting that for a normal person 'the question of sex comes in fourth or fifth place', Monsignor Escrivá added: 'Get used to pitching your struggle very far from the main walls of the castle'. And he used to issue the invitation to undertake 'a crusade of manliness and purity to counteract and undo the savage work of those who think man is but a beast'.

Putting these and so many other virtues into practice leads to 'peace and joy', he affirmed. Joy is the Christian's hallmark. Not the 'physiological "joy" of a healthy animal', but the joy that comes from the self-denial and surrender proper to God's children. 'This is a joy that cannot be taken away by anyone or anything because it has its roots in the form of a cross'.

This explains the unwaveringly positive approach of Monsignor Escrivá. He was always reminding Opus Dei members that they should be 'sowers of peace and joy' along all the paths of the world. 'Our Christian life must be inspired by optimism, joy, and the firm conviction that God counts on us'. For him Christian optimism is not a vacuous, cheery optimism, nor a blithe human expectation that everything will work out well. 'Rather, it is an optimism rooted in an awareness of our freedom and belief in divine grace. It is an optimism that leads us to be very demanding with ourselves and to make a real effort to respond to God's call'.

The Pope and the Church

'Christ. Mary. The Pope. Don't these three words sum up the loves that make up our Catholic faith?' So wrote Opus Dei's founder in 1934.

When he arrived in Rome for the first time, he lived in a tiny apartment from which it was possible to see the light in the window of the office where Pius XII worked. That whole first night Father Escrivá spent on the balcony praying for the Pope, to whom he felt so close. Successive popes were aware of and acknowledged this affection, backed up as it was by prayer and sacrifice. In a handwritten letter to the founder, Paul VI spoke of 'the fervent love of the Church and for its visible head that characterises' [Opus Dei].

The founder's veneration for Christ's Vicar led him to ask insistently for prayers for the Pope – 'whoever he may be'. It was the reason for his coming to live in Rome and for opening international education centres there. Thus he would 'romanise' his sons and daughters and the whole of Opus Dei. The move also manifested the Work's universality, already present in its foundational charism.

'What a joy to be able to say with all my soul: I love my Mother, the holy Church!' Many people who came close to Monsignor Escrivá confirm that he lived out this profound conviction to its ultimate consequences. He repeatedly offered his life as a sacrifice so that the Lord might bring to an end the trials besetting the Church. He inculcated this desire in Opus Dei members: 'Serve the Church as she wants to be served'. He also instructed them to be very united to the bishops in communion with the Apostolic See. He reacted against those who criticised the Church, especially if they were in some measure responsible for what they saw fit to criticise. Theirs was the serious injustice of 'making the wretchedness of some of the children appear to be faults of the Mother'.

MARRIAGE: A CHRISTIAN VOCATION

While upholding the Church's classical teaching about the intrinsic superiority of apostolic celibacy, Opus Dei's founder did open up a new way. 'More than once I have seen the eyes of men and women light up when they heard me say that marriage is a divine path upon this earth, whereas they had thought it impossible in their case to combine the giving of oneself to God and a human love that is noble and pure'.

For a Christian marriage is not simply a social institution and still less a remedy for human weakness. It is a genuine supernatural vocation that can and ought to be sanctified in all its aspects. God has given the body a share in his own creative power and has wished to use marital love to bring new beings into the world. Thus, Monsignor Escrivá affirmed that sexuality 'is not something shameful; it is a divine gift whose true purpose is life, love, fertility'. With this perspective, life in the family, marital relations, the care and upbringing of children, the effort to improve the material condition of the home, and relationships with other people are just so many ordinary human situations to which Christian couples are called to give a supernatural character.

Marriage and everyday life

The founder used to dream of 'bright and cheerful Christian homes' unaffected by the inevitable difficulties that arise, because mutual love would manage to overcome them. It is precisely when circumstances become difficult that self-giving and tenderness acquire deeper roots and really come into their own. To get across the practical implications of love between husband and wife, the founder, when he received couples, would sometimes ask the husband (and similarly the wife) if he loved his spouse to the point of loving even her faults. If the reply was negative (or more likely, hesitant), he used to remark that his love still had room to grow.

Furthermore, he would urge couples 'not to stem the sources of life, to have a supernatural outlook and the courage needed to bring up a large family', if God sent them one.

In his preaching, Monsignor Escrivá underlined the decisive role played by parents in the education of their children, a role that they cannot hand over to others, not even to teachers. The reason is that parents educate essentially through their behaviour. He encouraged them to make sure that their children from their earliest years could see them trying to live in accord with their faith. Then 'the child learns to have God among his first affections ... and learns to treat God as his Father and our Lady as his Mother'.

Respecting their children's vocation

The founder described the fourth commandment – honouring one's father and mother – as 'the sweetest precept of the Decalogue'. However, a son or daughter's freedom and duties can sometimes run counter to parental wishes. Parents should act as guides; they have a right to advise their children on career options, professional life, and choice of a state in life. But they should also respect whatever vocation God may give a child of theirs. Christians who are trying to sanctify themselves as husbands or wives because they are conscious of the greatness of their own vocation cannot but rejoice to see their children called to live apostolic celibacy.

Parents ought to resist any temptation to project their own ambition onto their children or to impose a preconceived plan on their lives. When Catholic parents fail to understand the vocation of giving oneself to God's service and that of souls, they have, in Monsignor Escrivá's mind, 'failed in their mission to form a Christian family. They are not even aware of the dignity Christianity gives to their matrimonial vocation'.

On the other hand, he was convinced that most children owe their vocation to their parents. He explained it like this: 'If you had brought them up to be criminals, they would be in prison. You have brought them up to be God's children, and God has claimed them. He has accepted your offer'.

PRIESTHOOD AND HOLINESS

Throughout his life Monsignor Escrivá took an extra-ordinary interest in the welfare of priests in view of their great influence for good or evil. He spared no effort in helping fellow priests and in preparing some of his sons for the priesthood. In his lifetime he himself led over one thousand men to the priesthood in Opus Dei.

Through the sacrament of Holy Orders, a priest is able 'to lend God his voice, his hands, his whole being', celebrating holy Mass *in persona Christi:* in the person of Christ. The priest is the direct and everyday instrument of the salvific grace Christ won for us on the cross. He is a special intermediary between God and man and a very important means by which man is sanctified. However, the priest cannot forget that he himself is also called to holiness, just as lay people are.

Priestly mission

Without in any way putting himself forward as an example, Monsignor Escrivá said of himself that he was a priest who spoke only of God. He felt this was the basic mission of every priest. As for Opus Dei members who were ordained after years of holding down an ordinary job, he used to remind them that they had become priests to serve and not to stand out or to give orders. Once they are priests they should leave their old profession behind and devote themselves entirely to their new 'professional work', to which 'they will dedicate every hour of the day, and still be short of time'.

While making clear that he did not know any bad priests (at most there were a few who were a little 'sick'), the founder did express his regret about some of them. 'There are some who, instead of speaking about God, talk about politics, sociology, anthropology. Since they know nothing about these things they get them wrong and moreover displease our Lord. A priest's ministry consists, instead, in making Jesus Christ's teachings known and administering the sacraments, helping people to seek Christ, to love Christ, to follow Christ. Anything else is just not their business'. This is the only way for priests to steer clear of rival factions; to act otherwise would be to betray Christ and to build a 'new' Church. When clerics substitute temporal goals for supernatural ends, they lose the people's respect and obedience and undermine the Church from within.

CONCLUSION

I hope this short survey of Opus Dei makes it easier to understand both its teaching and the life of its members. Opus Dei would never have become a spiritual catalyst in the modern world were it not for the extraordinary personality God gave Monsignor Escrivá. Ever faithful to divine inspiration, he 'sculptured' its spirit down to the last detail.

For Cardinal Koenig of Vienna, 'Monsignor Escrivá belongs to that select number of apostles, prophets, evangelists, pastors, doctors ... (cf. Eph 4:11) who have contributed in a remarkable way to the building up of the Body of Christ. The profound humanity of Opus Dei's founder reflects the character and concerns of our time.

'But his charism—that of someone set apart to carry out a special "work of God" – raised him to a higher plane. It projected him into the future. That is why he anticipated what were to be the great pastoral themes of the Church on the eve of the third millennium of its history'.

Furthermore, if in this changing world Opus Dei remains what its founder saw on 2 October 1928, it is because its members, equally called to be saints and apostles in the world, strive to achieve a unity of spirit, to be one with their Prelate and to welcome the on-going spiritual coaching that is part of their commitment. More than by reading the works listed in the bibliography that follows, it is through direct contact with Opus Dei members that one can best appreciate this solidarity.

It would not perhaps be presumptuous to suggest that we are witnessing one of the silent revolutions of which the Holy Spirit holds the secret. Opus Dei's importance to the Church and its implications for society are just beginning to emerge. Only time will show its full significance. As the founder said: 'Opus Dei will never have any problems adapting to the world, because its members are in the world. It will never have to catch up with human progress because its very members, side by side with other men and women living in the world, help to bring about this progress by their everyday work'.

Bibliography

Bernal S, *Mgr J Escrivá: A Profile of the Founder of Opus Dei*, Scepter, London 1977

Byrne A, *Sanctification of ordinary work: on the nature and spirit of Opus Dei*, Scepter, London 1985

Gondrand F, *At God's Pace*, Scepter, London 1989

Helming D, *Footprints in the Snow: a Pictorial Biography of Mgr J Escrivá*, Scepter, New York 1987

Illanes J.L, *On the Theology of Work: aspects of the teaching of the founder of Opus Dei*, Four Courts Press, Dublin 1982

Keenan W, *The Venerable Monsignor Escrivá*, Veritas, Dublin 1990

O'Connor W, *Opus Dei: an open book*, Mercier, Dublin & Cork, 1991

Seco L.I, *The Legacy of Mgr J Escrivá*, Sinag-Tala, Manila 1978

Thierry J.J, *Opus Dei: a close-up*, Cortland Press, New York 1975

West W.J, *Opus Dei: exploding a myth*, Little Hills Press, Australia 1989